SUZE ORMAN'S

FINANCIAL GUIDEBOOK

PUT THE 9 STEPS TO WORK

SUZE ORMAN'S FINANCIAL GUIDEBOOK

PUT THE 9 STEPS TO WORK

Suze Orman

THREE RIVERS PRESS • NEW YORK

Copyright © 1998, 2001, 2002 by Suze Orman

Published by Three Rivers Press, New York, New York. Member of The Crown Publishing Group, a division of Random House, Inc.

www. randomhouse.com

THREE RIVERS PRESS and the Tugboat design are registered trademarks of Random House, Inc.

Originally published for QVC as *Financial Freedom: Creating True Wealth Now* in 1998 and as *The 9 Steps to Financial Freedom Guidebook* in 2000.

Printed in the United States of America

Design by H. Roberts Design

CIP data is available on request.

ISBN: 0-609-80893-1

10 9 8 7 6 5 4 3 2

First Three Rivers Press Edition

How to Use Your Guidebook

With the aid of this guidebook, you will complete several interactive exercises to help you get in touch with and overcome your fears about money, as well as educate yourself about essential actions you need to take. The guidebook is what I consider a crash course in *The 9 Steps to Financial Freedom*. It highlights the most important concepts in that book. Please use it as a quick reference resource, a place to keep notes and record your thoughts, and a means to stay in touch with your financial habits and create an action plan.

The most critical steps on the path to Financial Freedom are the first two steps in the guidebook. Over the past few years, I have found that these two steps are the ones that most of you have difficulty with. To help make this journey easier, go to my Web site, www.suzeorman.com, where you will be able to access, free of charge, the audio program "Facing Your Fears & Creating New Truths," and hear these first two steps come alive. You will listen as approximately thirty people just like you go through these steps. Along with these people, you will laugh, cry, and make the connection from your past to your present, as well as break the chains of bondage that have kept you from having more and being more.

To access the audio program "Facing Your Fears & Creating New Truths," visit my Web site, www.suzeorman.com. Click on the icon "The 9 Steps to Financial Freedom Guidebook." Enter the username: **ask suze** and the password: **freedom.** Then download the audio program and listen away. Throughout Steps 1 and 2 you will see the following symbol ▭ . When you see this symbol, please know that it is a reminder that there is an audio program available to offer further assistance in completing the exercise you are being asked to perform.

Contents

This guidebook to the *9 Steps to Financial Freedom* offers a systematic approach that is divided into three sections. It is imperative that you do all the steps and do them in order.

   The first section takes us back to our most significant formative experiences with money. We revisit these experiences in order to understand why we do not always do what we know we should do when it comes to our money. Once we have achieved this understanding, then we are able to change not only our attitudes but our actions and start to create a life that is financially free.

The next section contains the Must-Dos to obtain Financial Freedom, as well as the Laws of Money. Here we will learn financial actions that we must take today to protect our tomorrows. We will learn about trusts and wills, credit card debt, saving for retirement, and the insurance we should and should not have. Most important, we will learn why it is so critical to trust ourselves more than we trust others, even the professionals to whom we are so accustomed to listening.

The last section takes us beyond money into an area of life that all the money in the world just can't buy. It is here that we learn the secrets of the money cycle and solve the mystery of money. With this last section we have entered the realm of Financial Freedom.

Financial Freedom: The Power Is Within You

WHAT DO YOU WANT FROM YOUR MONEY?

Financial Freedom is the pathway to inner and outer happiness, and the power to discover that pathway is within you. But first you have to know where you want that path to take you. You have to know what your goals are and in what direction you want to go. Not identifying your goals is like visiting a foreign city without a map, and without knowing what treasures are contained in that city. If you did this you would probably wander around the city aimlessly, maybe coming across the treasures, maybe not. Without financial goals and a road map to get you to them, it is highly probable that you will miss out on treasures that lie within your own financial city.

You purchased this guidebook for a reason, didn't you? Why? How did you think it was going to help you? In what way did you think it was going to guide you on your path to Financial Freedom? I want you to give some thought to your intention in buying this guidebook. To help yourself see your intentions clearly, ask yourself the following questions:

What do I want my ultimate financial destiny to be?
What do I want from my money today, as well as years from now?
What do I need to do to make my life worthwhile?

Please note that your intention should be long-range, what you want to see happen to you over the course of your life—not just today but for the next thirty or forty years. It is this intention that will help carry you through your entire financial life.

After you have given this some thought, please write your intention in the space provided below.

My intention in buying this guidebook:

_____

_____

_____

COMPLETION COMMITMENT

At important junctures throughout this guidebook, I will be asking you to make a written commitment to yourself to complete certain actions by a particular date or for a specific period of time. The 9 Steps to Financial Freedom can become a reality to you only if you complete the commitments I am asking of you. The first commitment starts right now, so please sign the commitment promise below, not going out further than six months from today before you commit yourself to completing all the exercises in this guidebook.

I promise to complete all the exercises in my Financial Freedom guidebook by:

_____   _____   _____
Date I will complete all   Signature   Today's date
exercises in my Financial
Freedom guidebook*

* Please go to your calendar now and write down the date by which you will complete all the exercises in your
   Financial Freedom guidebook.

All we really have in life to give to ourselves and to one another is our word. When we give it, we must never break it, for then we truly have nothing. Do not let the date you have just committed to arrive without having completed your commitment.

As you go through the guidebook, please use the checklist on the next page to mark off the actions you have completed. As you check off each action, you will start to feel a sense of accomplishment and power over your money. One of the goals of this guidebook is for you to have power over your money—rather than for your money to have power over you. At this point, you should have completed these actions: (1) intention in buying guidebook and (2) completion commitment, so please check off these two actions below. Throughout the guidebook you will see the checklist symbol ✔ as a reminder to come back to this list and check off the specific action you have completed.

THE 9 STEPS TO FINANCIAL FREEDOM CHECKLIST

_____ Intention in buying guidebook
_____ Completion commitment
_____ Goal-setting exercise

STEP 1

_____ Money messages exercise
_____ Think about your past
_____ Money memories exercise

STEP 2

_____ Embrace your fears
_____ Fear exercise
_____ One greatest fear
_____ Connect money memory and greatest fear exercise
_____ Creating a new truth exercise
_____ Reinforce your new truth
_____ New truth commitment

STEP 3

_____ Estimated average monthly costs
_____ How much is going out? exercise
_____ How much is going out? commitment
_____ Reality check on expenses
_____ How much is coming in? exercise
_____ Where do I stand?
_____ Three-step completion commitment
_____ Deciding how I choose to spend my money exercise

STEP 4

_____ People-first checklist
_____ What is stopping me from being responsible?
_____ Attorney worksheet
_____ Agents for durable power of attorney for health care
_____ How do I know if I or my life partner needs life insurance?
_____ How much life insurance do I and my life partner need?
_____ How long will I and my life partner need life insurance?
_____ Summarize your life insurance needs
_____ Review your policies yearly
_____ Term insurance quotes worksheet
_____ LTC insurance worksheet
_____ LTD insurance worksheet

STEP 5

_____ Are you repelling money? exercise
_____ Wallet exam
_____ Wallet checklist
_____ Do you have shame about credit card debt?
_____ Determine how much debt you have
_____ Rolling over a balance to lower credit card interest rate worksheet
_____ Borrowing to pay off debt
_____ Time and your 401(k) exercise
_____ Contributing to your retirement plan if you have credit card debt
_____ Commitment to contribute to retirement plan
_____ Time creates money quiz
_____ Put your money to work for you outside of retirement plans
_____ Are you making the most of your money?
_____ Money market account worksheet

STEP 6

_____ Do you have a financial advisor or a salesperson?
_____ What the advisor must ask you
_____ Where do you stand with your mutual funds?
_____ Mutual funds worksheet
_____ Investment quiz
_____ Dollar cost average worksheet
_____ How prepared are you to fund your child's college education?

STEP 7

_____ Do you repel money?
_____ Receiving exercise
_____ Giving experiment
_____ Are you attracted to generosity?
_____ Cheapskate quiz
_____ Giving commitment

STEP 8

_____ Ups and downs of money exercise

STEP 9

_____ What really matters
_____ How do you deceive yourself?

Setting Goals

So the question to you right now is: What is the goal that you want to achieve within the next year? Please note that there is a difference between your intention in buying the guidebook and your setting of goals that you want to achieve this year. Your goal is what you want to happen within one year. Your intention is the cumulative effect of all your goals. Defining your goal is something that you cannot skip over. So I want you to set a realistic goal now. There is nothing worse than setting a goal too high, where chances are you will not be able to attain it. It is nice to dream but this is not about dreaming—this is about creating a financial reality for yourself that can be attained within one year.

Here are some examples of realistic goals. Feel free to select one of these, rephrase it to fit your needs, or create one of your own.

I want to pay off my credit cards in full.
I want to invest $200 a month in a mutual fund.
I want to save enough money for a 20 percent down payment on a house.
I want to have the proper documents in place in case I die unexpectedly.
I want to have $3,000 to put toward my child's education.
I want to fund my Roth IRA to the maximum amount.
I want to take a year off and travel.
I want to stop fighting over money with my partner.
I want to get a better grasp on my expenses so I'm not always behind in paying my
     bills.
I want a job where I am making at least $50,000 a year.
I want to stop being afraid about money.
I want to pay off my student loan.
I want to give $100 a month to charity.
I want to be able to cover the costs of nursing home care so I won't be a burden to
     my children.

The most important thing to remember is that whatever your goal is, you can make it happen. Goal by goal, step by step, you can take charge of your destiny and achieve Financial Freedom. The power is within you.

GOAL-SETTING EXERCISE

Please ask yourself right now: What financial goal or goals do I want to attain by the end of this year? If you have more than one goal, list your goals according to priority. Write down your goals in the spaces provided.

Goal 1:

_____

_____

_____

Goal 2:

_____

_____

_____

Goal 3:

_____

_____

_____

Goal 4:

_____

_____

_____

As you accomplish your goals, continue to update them on a regular basis for yourself. By recording and updating your goals you will see just how far you've come.

✓

STEP 1

Seeing How Your Past Holds the Key to Your Financial Future

THE ROAD TO FINANCIAL FREEDOM

Financial Freedom begins not in a bank or even in a financial planner's office, but in your mind. It begins with your thoughts.

And your thoughts, more often than not, stem from your seemingly forgotten past with money. Please notice that I said "seemingly forgotten past," for in reality you have not forgotten your past at all. In my opinion, the reason that you don't do that which you know you should do with money has nothing to do with your capabilities. All of you are more than capable. It has to do with a memory that is connected with your early, formative experiences with money.

So, the first step toward Financial Freedom is a step back in time to the earliest moments you can recall when money first meant something to you. When you began to see that money could create pleasure—ice cream cones, merry-go-round rides—and could also create pain—fights between your parents, perhaps, or longings that couldn't be fulfilled because there wasn't enough money or even because there was too much. When you first understood that money was money. I want you to start to see how your feelings about money today (fearing it, enjoying it, loving it, hating it) can almost certainly be traced to an incident, possibly forgotten until now, from your past.

Suze's Money Memory

My earliest money memory goes back to when I was eight years old. In the hot Chicago summers, all of us in the neighborhood would go to the Thunderbird Motel to swim. It cost a dollar to get in. One Saturday, as usual, I said to my mom, "Can I have a dollar to go swimming?" And she said, "Sorry, Suze, but we don't have a dollar to give you right now. But don't tell your friends you don't have any money because if you do they will not like you anymore." I suddenly felt I was different from my friends, that I had less than they did, and that they wouldn't like me if they knew. After that night, once my mom and dad were asleep, I started to go into my father's pockets where he kept his money. I would take some bills out of his pocket—$1, $5, $10. I would take that money, not to spend on me, but to buy my friends gifts—a comic book, candy, a taffy apple.

Why did I start to do that? Because I wanted my friends to think I had money, for if I had money they would like me.

How long did I continue to do that? Until I was twenty or thirty years of age. I don't mean I continued to steal from my father, but I stole from myself in the form of taking my friends out to lunch, buying them gifts for birthdays, weddings, and holidays and charging it all on my credit card even though I didn't have the money to pay for it.

That one memory impacted many, many years of my life.

MONEY MESSAGES EXERCISE

Messages about money are passed down from generation to generation, worn and chipped like the family dishes. Your own memories about money will tell you a lot, if you take a step back and see how those memories influenced who you were—and whether those memories still influence who you are today.

In childhood we live full force. When you delve into childhood memories, they are vivid, alive with the experience of all the five senses—you can see, touch, taste, smell, and hear them. The smell of cotton candy from the local amusement park, the feel of wind against your face when you leaned out the car window, the mud squishing between your toes as you ran barefoot through mud puddles, the cold on your face when temperatures dropped below zero, the way your house smelled when your mother was cooking your favorite meal. I am asking you to look back into your childhood and remember everything you can about money, the wonderful things it did and the ways in which it might have scared you.

Remember back to when you were three, twelve, or seventeen, and see what comes up for you. When one money memory feels true and important, and keeps coming back, that's the one we want. Here are some questions to help you remember. Please answer yes or no.

	YES	NO
Did your friends have things that you didn't?	_____	_____
Did you feel that your friends had nicer clothes than you did?	_____	_____
Did your friends go on better vacations than you did?	_____	_____
Did you feel ashamed of having far more than your friends did, or far less than they did?	_____	_____
Did your mother have to work when other mothers didn't, or not have to work when others did?	_____	_____
Were you ashamed to bring your friends home to your house?	_____	_____
Did your friends' parents have more expensive cars than yours?	_____	_____
Did you hear your parents fight about money?	_____	_____
Did your mother hide things she bought because your father would yell?	_____	_____
Did you have to be extra good in order to earn special treats during your childhood?	_____	_____
Did you get money every time you went to see your grandparents?	_____	_____
Did you receive only money as gifts, instead of the personal touch of a hand-picked present?	_____	_____
Are there gifts you recall receiving as a child that were particularly special?	_____	_____
Did you steal from piggy banks, your parents' wallets, or the dime store?	_____	_____
Did you get less of an allowance than your friends or siblings got?	_____	_____
Did you have to work for your allowance or was it given to you as your right?	_____	_____
Did you get money for birthdays?	_____	_____
When you received money for birthdays, did someone tell you what to do with it?	_____	_____

✓

There is no right or wrong answer. This was just an exercise to help you remember your first money messages.

Think About Your Past 📼

As you are thinking back to your past, close your eyes. See whatever you can; remember what the scene looked like. What was happening in the scene? Was someone laughing, arguing, crying in the next room? With your child's eyes, and with the adult eyes you have now, picture everything you can remember. Here are some questions to help you.

Where were you?

_____

Was someone laughing, arguing, crying?

_____

What else was happening in the scene?

_____

How did it make you feel?

_____

This first step may open the floodgates to many emotions. I've done this exercise with hundreds of people, and most people—even those in the wealthiest families— recall a memory that leaves them still sad. The following are some examples of money memories. As you read these memories, think about your own life and your own money memory.

Tom's Money Memory

When Tom was nine his bike was stolen. His parents told him that he was irresponsible because he let it happen and that he did not know how to take care of what money could buy. Therefore he did not deserve to have his bike replaced—and in fact they never bought him another bike.

Sarah's Money Memory

When Sarah was twelve she asked her mother for a new dress to go to the school dance. Her mother told her she was selfish for wanting a new dress when they didn't even have the money to pay the bills. Sarah ended up not going to the dance because she felt she had nothing to wear, but she told all her friends she couldn't go to the dance because she was ill.

John's Money Memory

John remembers hiding in the backseat of his father's stretch limousine so his friends wouldn't see him. John had more money than all his friends and he didn't want to be different.

Anna's Money Memory

Anna received a smaller allowance from her father than her older brother and younger stepbrother did. This made her feel inferior and undeserving.

Every one of us has such a memory, and every such memory tells us at least part of the story of who we are today. If you let it, your memory will reveal the roots of the fears that so strongly rule your financial life. ✓

YOUR MONEY MEMORIES EXERCISE

OK, now it's your turn. Think about your past. Try to recall your earliest money memories, the ones that created the concept you have of money today. After you have spent some time thinking about this, you will find that one memory in particular feels true and important and keeps coming back. That's the one we want. Please do not censor yourself when you are doing this exercise. If more than one memory comes to mind, use the one that feels the most significant. I want you to be as specific as possible. I can't emphasize enough how important this exercise is. Please do not cheat yourself out of Financial Freedom by putting this exercise off or by not doing it at all.

Please write your money memories in the space provided.

_____

_____

_____

_____

_____

_____

_____

_____

_____

_____

Isn't it amazing how these seemingly innocent memories from our past can have such a pull on us as adults today? Now that you've completed this "Money Memories" exercise, I hope it's clear how large a role the mind can play in creating or destroying Financial Freedom. It's simply astounding to me how money memories have such a hold on our lives—how they directly impact whether or not we deal with our money in a healthy way. ✓

STEP 2

Facing Your Fears and Creating New Truths ▱

PART 1: FACING YOUR FEARS

We saw in the last step how powerful our memories of money from childhood are, even today. In this step we will hold these memories up against our fears. Then we will replace the habits of thought and action that our fears have created with strong new internal messages about what we will achieve with our money, beginning now. The sooner you deal with your fears, the more money you will be able to create. With money, when you heal your heart, you help your pocketbook.

From my years as a financial advisor I have learned that almost all of us have, at some level, fears or anxieties about money—but we rarely admit them to those around us. We may not even admit them to ourselves. Looking these fears in the eye is an essential step toward Financial Freedom.

Embrace Your Fears

Struggling to remember defines so much of our lives—to remember birthdays, dentist appointments, turning off the stove, where we put the keys, when the dry cleaning will be ready, what time the children need to be picked up—the rituals and obligations of everyday life.

Find yourself with a money problem, on the other hand, and often you just try to forget it. You can't. It will be with you day in and day out, at the movies, when you are trying to sleep, always there, never far from center stage of your consciousness. The fear is, very likely, powerful enough to keep you silent, too all-consuming to talk about, too big to take action against. Do you know that most of us push away fears without even knowing it? I am asking you now to step inside them, and pull them close for a moment.

So are you ready to do this? Are you ready to continue now and look into your fears, face them head on and see how money and your fears are related? To help you do this, here are some questions about your fears. Please check yes or no.

	YES	NO
Are you frightened that you won't be able to support your family?	_____	_____
Are you afraid that you can't keep up with your financial obligations?	_____	_____
Are you afraid of what others will think because your life partner makes more (or less) money than you?	_____	_____
Are you frightened that if your life partner dies, no one will be there to take care of you?	_____	_____
Are you scared that you will make a mistake with your money and you will lose everything you have?	_____	_____
Are you afraid that if your friends found out how much money you have, they wouldn't like you?	_____	_____
Are you afraid you are going to be audited by the IRS?	_____	_____
Are you scared because you don't even know the right money questions to ask?	_____	_____
Are you afraid that if your husband left you, you couldn't get by?	_____	_____
Are you afraid that you're never going to be able to fund your children's education?	_____	_____
Are you scared that your parents may have to go into a nursing home and there is no money to pay for their care?	_____	_____
Are you ashamed that you have to use your credit card just to cover the bills each month?	_____	_____
Are you afraid you'll have to support your spouse financially if you break up?	_____	_____
Are you afraid you won't ever be able to pay off your credit card debt?	_____	_____
Are you frightened of working until the day you die because you won't be able to sock away enough money for your retirement?	_____	_____
Are you scared by the thought of being homeless?	_____	_____
Are you scared that no one will be able to take care of you financially when you're old?	_____	_____
Are you afraid that you'll be fired and not be able to meet next month's bills?	_____	_____
Are you afraid that you'll never be able to afford to buy a house and therefore will have no place to call your own when you get older?	_____	_____

If you answered yes to most of the questions above, don't worry—most people answer yes. We have the exact same fears. However, there is a way to silence those fears—face them head on.

FEAR EXERCISE: WHAT IS IT THAT YOU ARE AFRAID OF? 🖭

   Ask yourself right now what it is that you are afraid of when it comes to your money. If nothing comes to mind, just give it time; often we block out what we don't want to face. Once you have identified your fears, write them down. (If you are having trouble identifying your biggest fears, visit my Web site, www.suzeorman.com, and listen to my audio program "Facing Your Fears & Creating New Truths." Directions on how to access the program are on page v.)
   My biggest fears are:

_____

_____

_____

_____
                                                                    ✓

   Look over what you have just written and select your one greatest fear about your financial life and summarize it in ten words or less. Please select just one fear. Write your greatest fear in the box below.

My one greatest fear about my financial life:

```
┌─────────────────────────────────────────────────────────┐
│                                                         │
│                                                         │
│                                                         │
│                                                         │
│                                                         │
│                                                         │
└─────────────────────────────────────────────────────────┘
```
                                                                    ✓

   How was that exercise for you? Was it a little harder than you thought? Or maybe easier? When I started to do these exercises for myself, it was amazing the things that I discovered.

Suze's Experience—Making the Connection
   Do you remember my money memory? My mother telling me that I shouldn't tell my friends that we didn't have any money, because if they found out they wouldn't like me? Well, do you know that one of my greatest fears in life as I got older was that if people found

out who I really was, they wouldn't like me because I didn't have money? This caused me to charge gifts for other people on my credit card so that it would appear that I had money and people would like me. My fear: If I didn't have money, no one would like me.

When I was able to see that this fear originated in a money memory from when I was eight years old, the chain of the past that was holding me back started to break. Do you see how it was very important for me to recognize the connection between the past and present? What we're going to do now is to help you make the connection between your money memory and your fear.

Below you will find a chart that lists some money memories, fears, and the manifestation of those fears. You'll notice that present-day fear and manifestation come from past money memories that share a common theme or words. Look closely at the money memories, present-day fears, and manifestations below, so you can understand how they connect. It is when you understand this connection that you will break the chains of bondage that keep you from being financially free.

CHILDHOOD MONEY MEMORY HIGHLIGHT	PRESENT-DAY FEAR AND HOW IT MANIFESTS
Suze's mother told her not to tell anyone that she did not have a dollar to go to the swimming pool, because if her friends knew she didn't have money, no one would like her.	SUZE'S FEAR: If I didn't have money no one would like me. SUZE'S MANIFESTATION: Suze charged gifts that she couldn't afford to give to her friends so it would appear that she had money.
When Tom was nine his bike was stolen and was never replaced because, his parents told him, he was irresponsible about the things that money could buy. He did not deserve to have his bike replaced.	TOM'S FEAR: I am totally irresponsible with regard to money and anything money can buy. TOM'S MANIFESTATION: Tom does not earn or save money, never buys himself anything, and lives like a pauper.
Anna received a smaller allowance from her father than her older brother and younger stepbrother did.	ANNA'S FEAR: I will never have as much money as others because I am not worthy of receiving it. ANNA'S MANIFESTATION: Anna never asks for a job promotion or pay raise and doesn't make as much money as she is capable of making.

Connect Your Money Memory and Your Greatest Fear Exercise 📼

This is a connect-the-dots exercise. I want you to revisit the past and trace your money memory to your greatest fear to see how the two connect to your life today. Please revisit the money memories that you wrote down on page 11 and write the highlights in the "Money Memory" column below.

Now take the greatest fear you wrote down on page 15 and write it in the "Greatest Fear" column.

MONEY MEMORY	GREATEST FEAR	HOW CONNECTED (KEY WORDS)
_____	_____	_____
_____	_____	_____
_____	_____	_____
_____	_____	_____

Can you see how these two are connected? What words are identical? What themes are identical? Please write what you notice in the "How Connected" column. Were you able to make the connection? Can you see your patterns? You might not at first. But over and over again I have found that when you examine your present-day fears, they're connected to your early memories. Understanding your fear often allows you to see what those memories mean.

If you haven't seen the connection, give it time. You've reopened your memories of money, long forgotten, and you've faced the fears long held inside you. The connection will come, too. This is a necessary step. So if you have not made this connection, put the guidebook down and visit my Web site, www.suzeorman.com, to access the audio program "Facing Your Fears & Creating New Truths." Directions on how to access the program are found on page v of this guidebook. ✓

PART 2: CREATING NEW TRUTHS 📼

It's great when you start to make the connections between your memories and your fears. Now you have to make sure those fears stay far away, because, if you let them, they will try to keep coming back. You have to retrain your mind away from thinking that you can't control money, that you don't deserve to do well, that not enough money is going to come in, that you don't have enough now, that you won't have enough tomorrow.

Believing, deeply *believing,* other realities makes other realities true: that you can control money, that you do deserve to do well, that there will be enough. How do you replace the old fears, the old reality? With new thoughts. With new truths. Your new truth will retrain your mind to believe that you can achieve your financial goals and will bring you much closer to realizing them.

Suze's Story

I grew up with the belief that pervaded our household: "We don't have any money. You'll always have to do without, so you had better learn how." I did learn how to do without—so you can imagine the shock I felt when I applied for a job as a stockbroker with Merrill Lynch in 1980 and was actually accepted.

Taking that job was breaking away from everything I had ever known. I was so out of my league. The most I had ever made was $400 a month as a waitress. I felt I didn't belong at Merrill Lynch because I thought I was less than everyone else. Remember, my mom told me so when I was eight years old: "Don't tell your friends, Suze, that you don't have money, because they won't like you." So I didn't think I belonged. Every morning I would get up and feel sick to my stomach, but off I would go with all these male stockbrokers in their three-piece pinstripe suits. When everyone else went to lunch at their fancy restaurants, I'd get in my car and go to Taco Bell. It was the only part of the day when I felt comfortable in my surroundings. The rest of the day, I thought I was just being a fraud.

The job itself was quite scary: telling people what to do with their money— and it was scary to have to make money just to keep my job. I went through a training program, but it didn't train me for the pressure, and it didn't give me the confidence I needed. I was a commissioned salesperson, and either I generated commissions or I would soon be looking for another job. It was a never-ending battle: Would I meet my quota each month, or would I be out on the street? I needed something to override the fear that was eating me alive. I decided to change my perception of my situation and create a new truth for myself.

I created what I wanted for myself on paper first. Every morning before I went to work, I would write over and over again: "I am young, powerful, and success- ful, producing at least $10,000 a month." Why did I write "at least"? Because why limit it? What if the world wanted to give me more? Why did I use the present tense? Because this was the life that I wanted to live in the present tense, not tomorrow, not someday. Now.

I wrote this new truth twenty-five times a day. And I just didn't write my new truth: I would sing it, scream it, and say it silently. I replaced the message of fear, and my belief that I was inadequate, with a message of endless possibility.

A few months after I created this new truth it started to become true. I started to feel powerful, I started to feel successful, and I started making over $10,000 a month. I was so excited that I sent a copy of my first $10,000 check to my mom. She thought I had made it up; she couldn't believe it. She told me, "Suze, nobody makes money like this." But her daughter was starting to make money like this. Now notice what just happened here. My mother told me that nobody made money like this. I could have chosen to believe her truth but instead I chose to believe my new truth. And your new truth can work for you, too, once you pull the fear out from wherever you've pushed it away to, face it, and use the power of your mind to put it behind you. Your new future continues with your new truth.

Creating a New Truth Exercise

The power of positive thinking is not a new idea, but when it comes to money it is new, because we're still so afraid of money. We're a culture of slogans—in ads, on bumper stickers, on T-shirts, needlepointed onto pillows. Call it what you like—a financial mantra, a new truth, an affirmation, a new belief in yourself—but you must create a positive, empowering message for yourself, a message of possibilities. Then take that powerful, positive message and plant it firmly in your mind to replace the fear you're leaving behind, beginning now.

THREE RULES FOR CREATING YOUR NEW TRUTH

1. Make your new truth short.
Your new truth needs to be short enough so that you can remember it exactly, word for word, and can say it in one sentence.

I have more money than I will ever need.
I am totally debt-free.
I am successful at managing my money.

2. Make it an unlimited truth.
Your new truth needs to be unlimited because sometimes we are meant to have more than we think we deserve. And we will tend to limit the amount of money that is meant

to come our way under the pretense of not being greedy or not asking for too much. To this day, I am very grateful that my new truth said that I was making at least $10,000 a month, for obviously more was to come my way.

> I am putting at least $200 a month into savings.
> I am making at least $10,000 a month.
> I have more than enough money to retire.

3. State your new truth in the present tense.
The reasons I want you to phrase your truth in the present tense is that I want you to focus your thoughts on today. If you say, "One day I will be financially free," this could mean twenty years from now. Your thoughts then go to the future and take you out of the present. Financial Freedom is attained by staying in the present. I learned this from Muhammad Ali when he was known as Cassius Clay. He came out and told the whole world that he was the greatest. He did not say, "One day I will be the greatest." He said, "I am the greatest." At the time he said it, it was not true. Shortly after that, it was.

> I am young, powerful, and successful.
> My future begins today.
> I am in control of all my money.

You can be your own financial champion with the aid of your new truth. Words are very powerful. They have the power to create or the power to destroy. The choice is up to you.

In the columns below, I have given you some examples of fears and new truths. Your new truth needs to be directly the opposite of your greatest fear.

GREATEST FEAR	*NEW TRUTH*
I will <u>never get out of</u> credit card <u>debt</u>.	I am totally <u>debt-free</u>.
I <u>hate dealing with my money and investing it</u>, and I believe I am <u>not capable</u> of doing it well.	I am skilled at <u>investing my money</u> and I love doing it.
I will <u>never</u> have <u>enough money</u> to support myself.	I have <u>more money</u> than I will ever need.

Write your greatest fear (the one that you wrote down on page 15) in the box below.

My greatest fear:

```




```

Now write your new truth in the box below. Remember to make your new truth the direct opposite of your fear. Make it short. Make it present tense. Make it unlimited.

My new truth:

```




```

If you're having trouble creating a new truth, visit my Web site, www.suzeorman.com, and listen to the audio program "Facing Your Fears & Creating New Truths." Directions on how to access the program are found on page v of this guidebook.   ✓

REINFORCE YOUR NEW TRUTH

Fear hates to be defeated. It will try to invade your new truth like a virus, telling you what you can't do, not what you can; telling you what you can't be, not what you are becoming; telling you what you aren't, not what you are and have every right to be. Don't listen. Just keep repeating your new truth. Remember, your new truth is bigger than your worries about the future, bigger than all the things you've meant to do with your money but haven't done. Your new truth is bigger than your credit card debt, bigger than your bank statements, and bigger than all your concerns for the future.

Keep your new truth close to your heart. Keep it front and center in your mind. If your old fear rears its ugly head, don't let it intimidate you. You can put it in its place. Use your new truth to counter your negativity. Say your new truth over and over again until your fear goes away. Soon, if you keep repeating your truth over and over again, your old fear will lose its power. It will lose its power to sway you, to keep you from succeeding and getting what you really want. By succeeding and getting what you really want, you will move closer to experiencing the pure joy of Financial Freedom.

I want you to start writing your truth twenty-five times NOW.

1._____
2._____
3._____
4._____
5._____
6._____
7._____
8._____
9._____
10._____
11._____
12._____
13._____
14._____
15._____
16._____
17._____
18._____
19._____
20._____
21._____
22._____
23._____
24._____
25._____

✓

New Truth Commitment

For the next six months, I want you to make a commitment to yourself.

1. I want you to say your new truth out loud twenty-five times as soon as you wake up in the morning.

2. I want you to get a notebook, and sometime during each day I want you to write down your new truth twenty-five times.

3. Right before you go to bed, I want you to look in the mirror and silently repeat your new truth to yourself twenty-five times.

Please do not neglect these exercises. They are designed to get you where you want to go, where you deserve to go. Before moving on to Step 3, please sign your commitment promise to yourself. Don't cheat yourself out of the experience of obtaining true Financial Freedom.

I promise to write and say my new truth twenty-five times a day, three times a day, for at least six months.

_____   _____ _____

Date six months from today   Signature   Today's date
when I will have completed
my commitment*

*Please go to your calendar now and write down the date until which you will continue writing and saying your new truth twenty-five times, three times a day.

✓

STEP 3

Being Honest with Yourself

GETTING IN TOUCH WITH YOUR MONEY

This third step toward Financial Freedom is about getting honest with yourself. In order to get honest with yourself, you have to get in touch with what you do with your money and understand that you have the power to decide how to use it. You have looked back to your childhood memories of money, connected them with your fears today, and created a new truth to keep the voice of those fears from paralyzing you against taking action. Now we are about to face your present reality. We will compare the money you have coming in with the money you have going out—real income, real expenses. With this step—your decision to face up to what you are really doing with your money—your thoughts, actions, and words about money will begin to merge and become truthful. With this step, you begin to take control of your finances in a concrete way.

Have you ever taken a big wad of bills from an ATM machine, then found yourself a day or two later nearly out of cash and unable to reconstruct exactly how you spent it? And even when you retrace all your steps, you still come up $20, $40, or $60 short? It's upsetting, but most of us feel that way most of the time: a little short, a little panicky, wondering exactly where our money is going. Why?

WE ARE ALL OUT OF TOUCH
WHEN IT COMES TO OUR MONEY

You see, everything about the way the money establishment functions is calculated to distance us from our money, to anesthetize us to its power. Think of the plastic card that slides through the machine so smoothly when we make our purchases, the automated voice of the bank's telephone answering system that robotically responds to our money questions, the digital electronic readouts of stock exchange information that flash on our TV screens. All of these conveniences leave us many steps removed from our money. And when we are removed from our money, we are rendered powerless and unable to protect ourselves against the things that can and do go wrong.

In order to protect yourself and those you love, and secure your future and theirs, you must first get back in touch with your money and understand that you have the power to decide how to use it. You have to start touching your money again. So many of us live by plastic alone that we don't even touch our cash anymore. We don't open up our bank statements. We may rely on someone else to handle our bills. In order to achieve Financial Freedom we need to begin to take control of our finances.

HOW IN TOUCH ARE YOU WITH YOUR MONEY? EXERCISE

Write down in the box below how much you think it costs you to live each month.

ESTIMATED MONTHLY AVERAGE COSTS:

I am willing to bet that after you complete this exercise, you will find that you do not know the real answer. How is that possible? Most of you believe, or deceive yourselves into believing, that all you need to live month in and month out is the amount of money you bring home in your paycheck. That is probably the figure you wrote down above. But you may shortly find that that is not your true cost to live. The reality, most likely, is that it costs you $500 to $1,500 more than that to cover all your expenses. Surprisingly, this discrepancy seems to vary only a little bit no matter what the income level. For example, if you wrote down that you think your average monthly costs are $3,000, I am willing to bet that after you do this exercise you will see that your costs are $4,000. Where does this month-to-month self-deception leave you? It leaves you totally unprotected, and eventually it leads you into financial chaos. ✓

WHERE THE MONEY GOES

The reason you probably don't know how much it really costs you to live is this: Your planned spending doesn't cover expenses that don't occur every month or expenses that just crop up occasionally. For example:

- Do you hold membership in a gym? If so, do you consider this cost by the month even if you pay your renewal fee just once a year?
- Do you wear disposable contact lenses? If so, do your estimated monthly expenses include the $40 the lenses cost you each month, or do you let yourself be surprised each time you have to buy a new annual supply for $480?
- Do you pay your insurance premiums twice or four times a year? Do you calculate the cost of insurance in your monthly bills?
- Did you go on vacation last year? How did that onetime expense average out over twelve months?
- Do you pay someone to do your taxes every year? How much does that come to per month?

- If you own a home, do you plan for the added expense of running your air conditioner in the summer and heating your house in the winter?
- If you have a fireplace, how many cords of wood do you buy each winter?
- If you hire a lawn service to care for your yard and garden, have you figured those seasonal weekly costs into your monthly budget?
- Did you send your children to camp last summer? And sign them up for skating lessons in the winter?
- Do you have pets? Do you have them groomed at least once each season? Take them to the vet a couple of times a year?
- Do you try to believe you spend little or nothing on clothes each year, when in fact you buy a few new things each season?
- Do you get your hair cut and maybe colored every couple of months?
- Do you go to the movies once a week? When you do, do you buy the tickets for yourself and your partner, have popcorn and sodas, or go for a simple dinner afterward?
- Do you take your partner out for an expensive anniversary dinner each year?
- How many birthday parties, housewarmings, weddings, and baby showers did you attend last year? Did you bring a present to each one?
- Do you know what the Christmas holiday season costs every year, and have you figured that amount into your monthly average?
- What about "small" expenses such as magazine subscriptions, cosmetics, supplies for the yard, oil changes for the car, batteries for the flashlight, charcoal for the grill?

These here-and-there expenses must also be considered so you know what it really costs you to keep your life running smoothly over a month's or a year's time. Once you take the step of identifying them, you will feel better for knowing the truth. And you will begin to gain power over the money that has controlled you for so long.

HOW MUCH IS GOING OUT? EXERCISE

I am asking you now to think about your money. Who cares more about your money than you? Shouldn't you know where it goes? It's one thing to say that you want to be financially powerful and responsible. But to to do that, you must face the truth honestly and know exactly where you stand today. This is essential.

Please get out all your canceled checks, ATM slips, credit card statements—whatever will tell you how you spent your money over the past year. These papers are more revealing than a diary; they contain the key to how much it really costs you to live your life.

> This exercise will take some time to do, but let's put time and money in perspective. You work at least forty hours a week to earn your money. I am asking you to spend a few hours taking your money out of the darkness, to see the light of reality, to see where you stand. Don't just read these pages. Pick up a pen and take action!

Instructions

1. Go through your bank statements, credit card statements—all the paperwork for the past year. If you don't keep your statements, this is your incentive to start.

2. Using the worksheet on page 30, record the amount that you spent monthly in each category. If there is a category relevant to you that is not listed in the worksheet, then add it in the blank spaces at the bottom.

3. After all the categories are complete, total each one in the column "Total Yearly by Category."

4. Then, for each category, divide the "Total Yearly by Category" figure by 12. This will give you how much you spend per month on average for that category. Write the figure in the column "Monthly Average by Category."

5. Now add together all the "Monthly Average by Category" figures and write this " 'Actual' Monthly Average Going Out for All Categories" at the bottom of the worksheet. This will tell you the average that it costs to live each month for all categories. Remember, you are working with averages. If your average is $3,000, most months you'll spend less—say $1,800 or $2,000—while in some months you'll spend $5,000 to $6,000. But $3,000 is the number you need to work from.

How Much Is Going Out? Commitment

Please do not continue in the guidebook until the "How Much Is Going Out?" exercise is completed. I am asking you now to make a commitment in the box below as to when you are going to complete this exercise.

I promise to complete the "How Much Is Going Out?" exercise by:

_____   _____   _____

Date I will have completed   Signature   Today's date
my "How Much is Going Out?"
exercise*

*Please go to your calendar now and write down the date by which you will complete this exercise.

Please note that if you're not willing to do this one little exercise, your true desire to obtain Financial Freedom is simply going to remain a desire. The completion of this exercise will allow you take the steps to turn your financial desire into a reality. If you are continuing in the guidebook, this assumes you have completed the exercise.

✓

HOW MUCH IS GOING OUT? WORKSHEET

	Jan.	Feb.	Mar.	April	May	June	July	Aug.	Sept.	Oct.	Nov.	Dec.	Total Yearly by Category	Monthly Average by Category (take the total yearly and divide by 12)
Mortgage/rent														
Property taxes														
Home maintenance/condo fees														
Home insurance														
Gas & electric														
Water														
Garbage removal														
Telephone/cellular phone														
Burglar alarm														
House cleaner														
Gardening														
Pool/spa														
Firewood														
Food/restaurants														
Medical/dental/optometric														
Veterinarian														
Insurance														
Auto expenses														
Tolls/parking/transportation														
Clothes/shoes														
Dry cleaning														
Jewelry														
Hair/manicure/facial														

Alimony/child support																								
Kids' school																								
Job training/education																								
Income taxes																								
Legal/accounting fees																								
Safe deposit box																								
Computers																								
Credit cards/loans																								
Bank/credit union fees																								
Express mail/postage																								
Books/subscriptions																								
Entertainment/video rentals																								
Cable TV																								
Sporting events																								
Vacations																								
Hobbies																								
Donations																								
Gifts																								
Lottery																								
Cigarettes																								
Miscellaneous																								

TOTAL "ACTUAL" MONTHLY AVERAGE GOING OUT FOR ALL CATEGORIES $

Reality Check on Expenses

Now I want you to take the " 'Actual' Monthly Average Going Out for All Categories" from the bottom of the worksheet on page 31 and write the amount in the first box below. Then, in the second box, write the "Estimated Monthly Average Costs" that you wrote down on page 26. Now take the "Actual Monthly Average Going Out for All Categories" and subtract the "Estimated Monthly Average Costs."

ACTUAL MONTHLY AVERAGE GOING OUT minus (−) ESTIMATED MONTHLY AVERAGE COSTS	$ $
DIFFERENCE (monthly deficit or excess)	$

Are you shocked by the difference between the two? If you are like most people, you will find that the result above is $500 to $1,500 higher than the figure you wrote down on page 26. If the figure is the same, congratulations. If there is a discrepancy, do you understand now how you have been deceiving yourself when it comes to your money? ✓

THE MONEY COMING IN

Knowing what is going out is only one part of getting honest with yourself. You also have to know if you have the money coming in to pay for what is going out. So now you are going to match exactly what you have coming in after taxes with what you have going out, on average.

HOW MUCH IS COMING IN? EXERCISE

On the worksheet below, I want you to write down all the income that you have coming in from all sources. Please calculate only the amount you are fairly certain will continue coming in for at least two more years. If you loaned someone money, for example, and she has been paying you back regularly but owes only three more payments, don't include this figure. Or if you're working and about to retire or be laid off, don't count the few paychecks you have left. Be as realistic as possible as to how much you can really count on, month in and month out.

INCOME WORKSHEET

	Yearly Amount
Yearly paychecks after taxes/deductions	
Predictable bonuses	
Social Security income	
Disability income	
Bond/interest income	
Interest income	
Dividend income	
Rental income	
Gifts from parents (if you can count on them)	
Loan repayments	
Pension income	
IRA income	
Miscellaneous	
TOTAL	$

Take the total above and divide it by 12. This figure is the average monthly amount you have coming in after taxes. Write the figure in the box below:

"ACTUAL" MONTHLY AVERAGE COMING IN: $

WHERE DO I STAND?

Now you will compare the difference between the amount coming in and and the amount going out on a monthly basis. Write the " 'Actual' Monthly Average Coming In" from page 33 in the first box below.

Then write the " 'Actual' Monthly Average Going Out for All Categories" from the bottom of page 31 in the second box.

Take the "Monthly Average Coming In" and subtract the "Monthly Average Going Out." This final figure, the difference of the two, represents a monthly sum that is in excess or deficit. Now you know exactly where you stand.

MONTHLY AVERAGE COMING IN	$
minus (–)	
MONTHLY AVERAGE GOING OUT	$
DIFFERENCE (monthly deficit or excess)	$

WHERE DO I GO FROM HERE?

If after completing the comparison above you discover that you have more than enough money coming in to pay your expenses, then you are doing fabulously and please skip to Step 4. But if you find that you have more going out than you do coming in—which is the case more often than not—you are left with two options:

• Make more money
• Choose how much you want to spend in each category

True Financial Freedom is attained by the combination of making more money and, at the same time, choosing how much you want to spend in each category. Notice my wording. I didn't say how much you are allowed to spend. I did not say to spend less. I said, decide how much you want to spend in each category. If you are spending more than you are earning, the solution is not about creating limitations. It's about making decisions as to what you most want to spend your money on. This does not mean that you have to take one drastic action that crimps your pleasures and quality of life, such as getting by with one car when your family needs two. Unrealistic budget cuts, like unrealistic diets, never work. Realistic budgeting means making wise choices; it does not mean deprivation.

DECIDING HOW I CHOOSE TO SPEND MY MONEY EXERCISE

This is how it works: Let's say that after you determine how much is going out and how much is coming in there's a shortfall of $8,000 a year. Rather than take drastic measures, like cutting out your family vacation and selling the second car, decide in what categories you want to shave your expenses. There will be some categories where the amounts are fixed—rent, mortgage, insurance, taxes, and so on. There will be other categories—in fact, the majority of categories—where you can decide what the total spent per year will be. You can almost make a game of it with yourself. If you have your hair cut and colored every eight weeks, see if you can schedule it for every nine weeks. You'll save the cost of one whole haircut each year and probably won't notice any difference in your appearance. Is there one magazine subscription you can do without? Can you have three Friday movie nights a month instead of four (or five, in the months with five Fridays)? Can you have your windows cleaned every eight months instead of every six months? Keep deciding to trim, a little here, a little there, until what comes in matches what goes out. Keep your new truth with you as you begin to consider how you want to spend your money. With each decision you make, you are gaining power over your money.

TRIMMING TIPS

You may find that you can come up with wonderfully creative ways to trim your spending so that you hardly notice. The following is a list of some actions people have taken to painlessly trim some money from different categories.

Action	Yearly Savings
Make your own coffee in the morning rather than go to Starbucks	$850
For insurance and DMV registration savings, purchase a used car rather than a new car	800
Carpool to work	750
Rather than buy new CDs, trade with friends for CDs you don't have	600
Do taxes with a computer program rather than hire an accountant	600
Do your own manicures	500
Buy generic drugstore items (like aspirin, toiletries) rather than brand names	500
Return videos on time	250
Wear clothes one more time before dry cleaning	250
Stop using cell phone for local calls	200
Buy Christmas trimmings, cards, and wrappings in January at 50% off	100

Only when you see clearly exactly how you spend your money will you be able to decide how you would rather be spending your money.

Instructions

1. On page 38 there is a worksheet, "How I Choose to Spend My Money." In the first column, "How Much Went Out Last Year," write down the yearly information that you listed on the worksheet "How Much Is Going Out?" on pages 30–31.

2. Now it's time for you to take control of your money by filling in the next column, "How Much Will I Choose to Spend This Year?" Since you know how much you overspent last year, decide where and by how much you are going to cut back. Or, if you don't need to cut back, reallocate funds to a category in which you would rather be spending your money.

3. Each month when you pay your bills, track your spending in each category by filling in the monthly columns on the chart. You might challenge yourself to spend less than the maximum amount you've chosen and build up your savings. If you use up any allocation early and want to spend more in that category, you'll have to make new decisions about what, if anything, you want to do by seeing where you stand with the other categories. In other words, you can rob Peter to pay Paul, except that you're Peter and you're also Paul.

4. Say you decided you want to spend $2,000 this year on clothes. But in November you find a $200 coat you want, after the $2,000 has already been spent. Before buying the coat or deciding to go without, check your other categories. Maybe you can choose to cut your holiday vacation short and save $200. As long as the numbers always balance, you're in the driver's seat.

5. It's important to be flexible. You might decide midyear that you miss your Friday night dinners on the town and would rather forfeit a few movies. You can deduct money from one category and add it to another and keep reorganizing how you spend your money as the year proceeds. Please try and allocate an extra $50 to $100 each month for miscellaneous unpredictable expenses, such as medical bills not covered by your insurance. There is no way to avoid such surprise costs, so you need to figure them in.

REVIEW

At this point you have taken the first steps to Financial Freedom. You have connected your money memory and the fear that has kept you from dealing with your money. By creating and reinforcing your new truth you have started to rediscover the power and strength that enable you to be in control of your money—the money you have now and the money that will come to you. You've gotten honest with yourself financially and are at a point where you can choose what you want to spend money on and what you don't. You do not need a budget to limit what you can spend each month. Rather than being dictated by a restriction, your actions are dictated by the choices you make. You are able to juggle your money to where you want to spend it rather than where it wants to be spent.

For those of you who haven't done the exercises, my question to you is, what is stopping you? Please don't deprive yourself of all you were meant to have. It is not enough to simply read about the steps to Financial Freedom, you must take action. Before reading further, if you have not completed all the exercises go back to where you stopped and start again. If you have not completed these first three steps in totality nothing else will work. Please recommit to completing the first three steps before moving on to Step 4.

Three-Step Completion Commitment

I promise to complete Steps 1, 2, and 3 before moving on to Step 4.

_____ _____ _____
Date I will have completed   Signature   Today's date
Steps 1 through 3.

✓

For those of you who have completed all the exercises in Steps 1 through 3, congratulations. You have just taken the hardest steps toward Financial Freedom. Please move on to Step 4.

HOW I CHOOSE TO SPEND MY MONEY WORKSHEET

	How Much Went Out Last Year?	How Much Will I Choose to Spend This Year?	Money Spent in Jan.	Money Spent in Feb.	Money Spent in Mar.	Money Spent in April	Money Spent in May	Money Spent in June	Money Spent in July	Money Spent in Aug.	Money Spent in Sept.	Money Spent in Oct.	Money Spent in Nov.	Money Spent in Dec.
Mortgage/rent														
Property taxes														
Home maintentance/ condo fees														
Home insurance														
Gas & electric														
Water														
Garbage removal														
Telephone/cellular phone														
Burglar alarm														
House cleaner														
Gardening														
Pool/spa														
Firewood														
Food/restaurants														
Medical/dental/optometric														
Veterinarian														
Insurance														
Auto expenses														
Tolls/parking/transportation														
Clothes/shoes														
Dry cleaning														
Jewelry														
Hair/manicure/facial														

Alimony/child support	
Kids' school	
Job training/education	
Income taxes	
Legal/accounting fees	
Safe deposit box	
Computers	
Credit cards/loans	
Bank/credit union fees	
Express mail/postage	
Books/subscriptions	
Entertainment/video rentals	
Cable TV	
Sporting events	
Vacations	
Hobbies	
Donations	
Gifts	
Lottery	
Cigarettes	
Miscellaneous	

TOTAL "ACTUAL" MONTHLY AVERAGE GOING OUT FOR ALL CATEGORIES $

STEP 4

Being Responsible to Those You Love

ALL THE WHAT-IFS

A big part of financial freedom is having your heart and mind free from worry about the what-ifs of life. Each of us—from those who wish creditors would stop calling, to those with millions of dollars—has to face the what-ifs. When you consider taking actions to protect yourself and those you love, it is not enough to say you will "get to it" or to think fuzzily that you already have gotten to it. It is essential to get to it now and know you have planned and prepared in the best way possible. The fourth step to Financial Freedom is being responsible to your money as well as to those you love.

It is not nice when you get sick or when you die to leave those you love not only in emotional chaos but in financial chaos as well. It will be hard enough for those around you to bear the grief of your illness or death. Imagine for a minute their pain. Please don't force them to deal as well with all the matters you could have taken care of while you were alive and healthy.

> **THE FIRST LAW OF FINANCIAL FREEDOM:**
> People First, Then Money

When you have taken care of others and put people first, you have responded to the higher values of your existence: people first, then money. It's as if, on a material level, you're giving thanks by taking care of those who helped you enter the world, those to whom you gave life, those who have guided your passage through your life. By taking caring actions, you remind yourself of who you really are and what is important to you—what is important in this life. This knowledge is a powerful force. I think it is almighty. The force starts to push forward like a bulldozer, clearing away all the obstacles that prevent you from living the life you deserve to live. As you complete the rest of the steps in this guidebook, these obstacles will continue to be cleared away. Unlikely as it may sound to you now, you will be closer and closer to paying off your Visa bill, taking that trip to Italy, or whatever your goal happens to be.

PROTECTING OTHERS

It is essential that you have documents in place that protect you and those you love in case of the what-ifs. If something were to happen to you right now—a life-threatening illness or an early, unexpected death—are all your financial affairs in order? If you answered yes, are you sure?

Do you have the following updated documents in place? Please check yes or no.

PEOPLE-FIRST CHECKLIST

	YES	NO
Up-to-date will	_____	_____
Revocable living trust with an incapacity clause	_____	_____
Up-to-date durable power of attorney for health care	_____	_____
Proper life insurance	_____	_____
Proper disability insurance	_____	_____

If you checked yes for every item, I congratulate you, for you are truly coming from a place of protecting others and yourself.

If you do not have the correct documents in place, you have to ask yourself, why not? What is stopping you? Please answer the question below:

What is stopping me from being responsible and protecting myself and those I love when it comes to money?

_____

_____

_____

_____

_____

_____

Look at the reasons you wrote down. Do your reasons truly make sense? There is no excuse that is valid if Financial Freedom, combined with being responsible to those you love, is really your goal.

If you do not have the correct documents in place or do not even know where to begin to get your documents, do not be overwhelmed. In this step I will explain the importance of these documents and how to go about getting them.

The first step in being responsible and protecting others is to make sure that you have a will and—in most cases—a revocable living trust. Remember, it is not *if* you are going to die but *when* you are going to die. The following section is devoted to what you need to know about these two essential documents. The information is presented in a question-and-answer format to make it easier for you to refer to this information when you go to create a will and/or a revocable living trust.

Wills

What is a will?

A will is a legal document that states to whom you want your assets to go after your death. Even so, the title to your property will not automatically transfer to your designated beneficiary after your death without first going to probate court, which is a lengthy and costly procedure. (The language of wills and trusts may seem daunting. Please see page 56 for a rundown of terms you need to know.)

What is probate?

Probate is a court procedure in which the judge has to authenticate your will and make sure it is valid. Then he or she will sign the titles of all your property over to the appropriate people. Sounds simple, but in some states this process can take six months to two years and can be quite expensive. Take California, for example:

Estate Size	Probate Fee, California*
$100,000	$ 6,300
200,000	10,300
300,000	14,300
400,000	18,300
500,000	22,300
600,000	26,300
750,000	32,300
1,000,000	42,300
1,200,000	46,300

*Combined basic fees for court, executor, and attorney.

What is a probate affidavit?

If your estate is small, from $10,000 to $100,000 (depending on the state), you might be able to avoid probate with a simple will and a process called probate affidavit. It costs very little, doesn't take much time, and makes it easy for your survivors to receive what you want them to. Probate affidavit forms are available in most banks at no cost. Be careful, though. Your estate could be worth more than you think.

How do I get a will?

There are a few ways you can do this. You can have a lawyer draw one up. This should cost from a hundred to a few hundred dollars, depending on where you live and how complex your affairs are. You can buy a form will, which should cost about $10, at a stationery store and fill in the blanks. Or you can get a computer program that will generate a will for you for about $35. If you use any of these methods to draw up your will, you'll also need to sign it and, while you are signing it, have two or three people witness your signature and then sign the will, too. Most states require two signatures, a few three, so to be on the safe side, ask three people to witness your signature.

What if I want to make a change to my will?

When you want to change anything in your will, you simply draw up what is called a codicil, which is an additional piece of paper enumerating your changes. Follow the same procedure, including using witnesses, as you did when you signed the will in the first place.

What is a holographic will?

A holographic will is a will you write by hand on a piece of paper; it costs you nothing. Just make sure that the paper you use has no other writing on it or the will will not be considered legal. Make sure, too, that the entire will is in your handwriting and is dated and signed by you. If you make a mistake, don't cross it out. Start over. Anything crossed out is considered an interlineation, making the will null and void. Do not have anyone else witness a holographic will because, again, this will make it null and void. If you want to change a holographic will, you must redo the entire thing.

Can wills be contested?

Yes. Anyone who thinks he or she should have something that the deceased left to someone else in the will has the right to come to the court and ask for it. Then the judge has to decide. Also, although people commonly use wills to specify the guardians they want for their children, their recommendation is not binding. It can only express their wishes.

What if I don't have a will?

No problem, as long as you don't die.

    If you do die —and it's not "if" you're going to die, it's "when" you're going to die—

your loved ones will soon find that by not taking action, you have left their inheritance up to the state.

Let's say you own your house, which was part of your divorce settlement, in your own name. Since divorcing, you've remarried, and you are hopelessly in love with your new hubby. Still, because of the terrible divorce you went through, you feel a little safer keeping the house in just your name. Your two children from your first marriage have never liked the idea that you remarried, and even though they're grown, they're extremely possessive of the house they grew up in. If anything were to happen to you, you want your new husband to be able to stay in the house for as long as he likes. The title would then transfer to your kids. But you haven't gotten around to creating a will or a trust.

One day on your way home from work, you're killed in a car accident. Because you have no will, the laws of the state go into effect with a process called "intestate succession." According to state law, your husband will own half the house, and your kids (who do not approve of him at all) will own the other half. If they wanted to, they could force him to sell his home. If nothing else, they could probably make him buy out their half—that is, if they're willing to give up their attachment to the house. In any event, they'll all have to go to court and come up with the money to pay the court fees.

Trusts

What is a revocable living trust?

A revocable living trust is a document stating who controls your assets while you are alive and what will happen to the assets when you are gone. It's called a trust because you are trusting this entity to take care of your assets for you and to carry out your wishes when you can no longer do so for yourself. It's called "living" because the trust is going to be set up while you are alive and will also live on after your death to carry out your wishes. "Revocable" means that whoever creates the trust can change it at any time.

How is a revocable living trust different from a will?

While a will states where you want your assets to go after your death, it takes effect only with a court order. With a revocable living trust you take the steps while you are alive to sign the title of your property over to the trust, which functions for your own use and benefit while you are alive and lets you specify where you want each piece of property to go when you die. While you are alive the property is held in the name of the trust for you. When you die the trust passes your property directly to the people you want to have it. The trust lives on even after you're gone, carrying out your wishes. Anytime you want to, you can amend the trust, so you can always change your mind about who gets what. Most important, with a trust, there is no probate. The courts are not involved in the transfer of your estate. (See also the quick reference guide "Will Versus Revocable Living Trust," page 52.)

What is the cost of a revocable living trust?

Depending on the size of the estate, you should be able to get a simple revocable living trust drawn up for between $500 and $3,000. If you decide you want your attorney to fund the trust—that is, to transfer your assets into it—it may cost you more. Once the trust is set up, making simple changes to it should cost about $100. Obviously, fees will vary depending on where you live and how complex your requirements are.

What is "funding" a trust?

By itself, the document establishing the trust means nothing until the trust assumes ownership of the things you intend to put into it. Once the trust has been set up, in other words, your assets must be transferred into it. This means that if John and Jane Doe owned a house together in their own names, after they established their trust they would have a new deed issued that would list the owner as John and Jane Doe, trustees for the John and Jane Doe Revocable Living Trust. The Does would also change the titles on their bank accounts, stock portfolio, and so on. Doing this is simply a matter of paperwork. Computer programs and books about trusts provide sample letters to show you how to fund your trust. If you have a lawyer draw up your trust, he or she will have form letters available to show you. Or the lawyer can handle changing the titles for you; even if the fee is higher than that for simply drawing up the trust itself, it might be well worth it—different institutions have different requirements for making the change. A thorough attorney will also update the beneficiary designations on your life insurance policies and your IRAs and other retirement accounts and coordinate them with the trust.

How do you provide for children with a trust?

Particularly when you have children, the earlier you do your revocable living trust the better, even if you don't have a lot of money. If your children are very young and anything should happen to you, they may be at much greater risk than you can imagine. A will can only express your wishes. The court always has the last decision when it comes to who is appointed legal guardian of your children. For instance, if your children are under eighteen, and all you leave them is a life insurance policy, a guardianship for those assets is created upon your death, naming the executor or someone else as the guardian for the money. Each year the guardian has to go back to court to account for the money spent on behalf of the children during the past year. When each child reaches eighteen, regardless of his or her ability to handle the money on his or her own, each child's share will be legally signed over, lock, stock, and barrel to him or her. By the time the children get it, there will not be as much as there could have been, either, because every year there will have been guardian fees and fees to a lawyer to do the guardianship reporting.

If you die with a trust, on the other hand, the courts still have the final say over guardianship of the person, but you can make the important decision of how, when, and for what purposes your children will receive the money you are leaving them. You assign a successor trustee (your chosen guardian, for example)—or two or three or however many you like—and specify when you want your children to receive their money and how you'd like that money to be used until that time, and poof, it's done. The successor trustee(s) can take care of your children's financial lives on your behalf. No yearly reporting, no fees, no nothing.

Think trusts are for old people who are likelier to die? Think again. Trusts are for people who are lucky enough to live among people they love. Trusts are for people who are responsible to those they love.

If I have a revocable living trust, do I need a will?

Just because you have a trust does not mean you don't need a will. It is very important to have a will as a backup, covering any assets you have not put into your trust—things such as furniture, personal items, and items of strictly sentimental value. If you have underage children, you should designate the person you want to serve as their guardian so your wishes will be clear to the court. A trust does not address guardianship.

If you have not created a will or a trust, or worry that you haven't done it properly, then you should make time within the next few weeks to see an attorney who specializes in drawing up these documents. If you already have a will and/or revocable living trust, when was the last time you looked at it? Is it up-to-date? Take it out now and look at it and make sure that nothing needs to be changed.

Do I need an attorney to draw up a revocable living trust?

Not necessarily. There are books and computer programs that you can purchase to do this on your own. Nolo Press is a good source of materials. You can visit its Web site, www.nolo.com, and research this for yourself. But with that said, even if you do the preliminary work and the drafting of the documents yourself using books or computer programs, you should have the documents reviewed by a trust attorney to make sure that you have done the work properly. I sincerely believe this is one area in which professional help *should* be sought.

My attorney told me probate is cheaper than a revocable living trust. Is that true?

Do you remember those probate fees I mentioned earlier? Well, some of them get paid to your executor and to your attorney. So, in most states, attorneys stand to profit from your having only a will and not a revocable living trust. This may be one reason why your attorney has told you that probate is cheaper.

Also keep in mind that your attorney may not be an estate specialist and may not be familiar with all the benefits of trusts. Ask him how many trusts he has prepared in the last three months and how many allocation agreements for A-B trusts (see page 50) he has prepared. If he looks at you as if you are speaking Greek, politely get up and leave. To prove the point, I want you to ask your attorney to estimate for you, in writing and on his or her letterhead, the following:

1. how much it would cost you to have a will drawn up, if you don't already have one;
2. how much it would cost your beneficiaries to probate your entire estate (including court costs and attorney and executor fees) if you and your spouse died today with wills alone;
3. how much it would cost to create and fund a revocable living trust;
4. how much it would cost your beneficiaries to settle your estate if you and your spouse died today with that revocable living trust.

Add the cost of drawing up each document to the respective cost to your beneficiaries after your death and compare the two totals. The option that costs less is the one your attorney should recommend. If the calculations suggest that you would be better off with a trust, and you've been told it's unnecessary, you may need to get a new attorney. (See below for suggestions on finding a good will-and-trust attorney.)

If the calculations suggest that you do not need a trust and your attorney can clearly explain this to you, be sure to review your financial status and the relevant laws every few years to be sure that having only a will still makes sense. And make sure you give a copy of the document stating your attorney's estimates to your beneficiaries so that when this hypothetical event becomes a reality your beneficiaries will hold the attorney to the estimated costs.

How do I find a good will-and-trust attorney?

The hardest part of creating a will and trust is finding a good will-and-trust attorney. Word of mouth is the age-old way of finding an attorney, so ask your friends, but please make certain you find an attorney well versed in estate planning. You may want to contact your local university, especially if it has a law school. Call and ask a professor who specializes in estate planning whom he or she would recommend. There are two other sources that I would consider. The first is:

The American College of Trust and Estate Counsel
3415 South Sepulveda Boulevard, Suite 460
Los Angeles, CA 90034
(310) 398-1888
(310) 572-7280 (fax)
www.actec.org

Or you can consult the *Martindale-Hubbell Law Directory,* available at your local library or on the Internet at www.martindale.com. This is a comprehensive nationwide listing of lawyers, and it will have the names and addresses of all the lawyers in your state.

When you do get the names of some attorneys, please make sure you interview at least three of them. Attorneys expect this, so there usually is no fee for going through this process with them. An attorney plays a major role in making sure your estate is set up correctly, and your survivor will need his or her assistance after your death. You want to make sure that not only you but those around you like this lawyer and feel comfortable in his or her presence. So take your family members to these interviews.

During the interview, what questions should I ask the will-and-trust attorney?

You should ask your prospective attorney the following questions and get the following answers. If you get a different answer, you don't have the right attorney.

How long have you been specializing in estate planning?
The answer should be at least ten years.

How many people have you drafted wills and trusts for in the past five years?
The answer should be at least two hundred people.

Will you be drafting the documents yourself or will someone else be doing the paperwork?
It is OK if someone else draws up the paperwork if that person is supervised correctly. This may cost you less. You just need to know one way or the other.

How much do you charge?
You want the attorney to charge a flat fee to draw up a will and/or a trust. The fee should include drawing up the document and explaining it to you (which could take a few hours if it is a trust) as well as funding the trust (doing the paperwork to transfer the titles on all your property and assets into the name of the trust).

If I have other questions, will you charge me if I call and ask?
There should be no charge for simple questions over the phone.

On page 57 you will find a worksheet to use when you are interviewing prospective attorneys. Remember you need to interview at least three attorneys before you decide.

Does the trust attorney I use have to be located in the state in which I reside?

Not necessarily. But your trust attorney does have to be licensed in the state in which he or she works. Let's say, for example, that you live in Wisconsin but locate an attorney you trust in California. You can meet with that attorney, either by phone or in person in California, and he or she can perform the work for you in California and mail or fax it to you in Wisconsin. If the attorney isn't licensed in Wisconsin, however, what he or she can't do is go to Wisconsin and do the work there.

Will a revocable living trust help me with estate taxes?

A revocable living trust will not help on any level with the estate taxes above the unified credit exemption. A revocable living trust is meant primarily to avoid probate fees, to transfer legal title to your assets as quickly as possible to beneficiaries, and to protect you when you become incapacitated.

What is the unified credit exemption?

It is the amount that your beneficiaries can inherit without having to pay federal estate taxes:

For Deaths Occurring In	Highest Estate Exemption	Highest Estate- and Gift-Tax Rate
2002	$1,000,000	50%
2003	1,000,000	49
2004	1,500,000	48
2005	1,500,000	47
2006	2,000,000	46
2007	2,000,000	45
2008	2,000,000	45
2009	3,500,000	45

Due to recent changes in the tax law, beginning in 2002 estate taxes are being phased out over nine years. Ultimately, if you die in the year 2010, there is no estate tax and the top gift-tax rate will be equal to the highest individual income-tax rate (scheduled to be 35 percent) with a $1,000,000 unified credit exemption. But please keep in mind that in 2011, unless new legislation is passed, the Economic Growth and Tax Relief Reconciliation Act of 2001 will expire and estate taxes and the highest unified credit exemption will be reinstated at the 2001 rate.

Is there any trust that reduces estate taxes?

Yes, you can have an A-B trust (also known as a tax-planning trust, a credit shelter trust, a marital trust, or a bypass trust).

What is an A-B trust?

An A-B trust is used primarily by married couples. It is a trust created while both spouses are alive. When one spouse dies, the trust is normally split into two shares, an A share and a B share. One share remains a revocable trust and the other becomes an irrevocable trust, meaning that that portion of the trust cannot be changed. A-B trusts should be considered if you are married and have assets in excess of the unified credit exemption amounts listed above. An A-B trust established while you and your spouse are alive essentially allows you to double the money you leave to your beneficiaries without incurring estate taxes, depending on how you hold title to your assets and how much each of you owns. Otherwise, your beneficiaries are limited to the unified credit exemption for the year of your death. Any amount inherited above the exemption will be subject to an estate-tax rate that begins at 37 percent and goes as high as 50 percent in 2002. (The top rate will drop to 49 percent in 2003, and keep dropping until it reaches 45 percent in 2007. But beware: The top rate may rise again starting in 2011.) For further illustration of how an A-B tax planning trust works, please see the graphs on pages 54 and 55.

What is the difference between an A-B trust and a revocable living trust?

A revocable living trust is meant primarily to avoid probate fees, to transfer the legal titles to your assets as quickly as possible to your beneficiaries, and to protect you if you become incapacitated. An A-B trust can save your beneficiaries significant estate taxes if you are married and expect to have an estate valued at more than the allowable nontaxable amounts. For a comparison between A-B tax-planning trust and revocable living trust, please see the quick reference guide on page 53.

Is there a limit to the amount of assets a husband and wife together can shelter in an A-B trust?

Yes. Here are the maximum amounts for federal estate credits for current and future years:

For Deaths Occurring In	Maximum Estate Credit
2002–2003	$2,000,000
2004–2005	3,000,000
2006–2008	4,000,000
2009	7,000,000
2010	Unlimited

Is an A-B trust just for married couples?

Unmarried heterosexual couples, same-sex couples, or any two people can set up A-B trusts that will remain in place until both partners have died. The tax benefits will go to those who receive the assets after both partners have died. But there is no tax deferral for unmarried couples comparable to the unlimited marital deduction between spouses. So if your joint estate exceeds the maximum estate credit above, avoiding tax on the first partner's death is possible only if you are married. Only married couples can take advantage of the unlimited exemption between spouses.

QUICK REFERENCE GUIDE: WILL VERSUS REVOCABLE LIVING TRUST

	WILL	REVOCABLE LIVING TRUST
What is the difference?	A will is a legal document that states where you want your assets to go after your death.	A revocable living trust is a legal document that states who controls your assets while you are alive and what will happen to them when you're gone. You take the steps while you are alive to sign the title of your property over to the trust for your own use and benefit while you are alive. When you die the trust passes your property directly to the people you want to have it.
Who should have one?	Everyone should have a will. If you die without a will, the state, not you, will decide how your property will be distributed and to whom.	I also believe everyone should have a revocable living trust. You should have one especially if you own property or other assets, have children, or care about what happens to the people you love after you are gone.
Can my beneficiaries inherit my estate without going through probate?	No. A will does not avoid probate in most cases. After your death, your designated beneficiaries in most cases must go to probate court to have a judge assign title of your estate. Probate court is a lengthy and costly procedure. In the state of California, for a house valued at $200,000 (regardless of the mortgage) your beneficiary will have to pay a statutory probate fee of $10,300.	Yes. With a trust there is no probate fee for your beneficiaries to pay. When you die the trustee passes your property directly to the people you want to inherit it. The courts are not involved.
How do I get one?	If you want to prepare a will yourself, there are books that show you how, computer programs that will generate one for you, and fill-in-the-blanks forms that you can purchase in an office supply store. If you decide to do it yourself, I urge you to have a qualified attorney look it over to make sure you did it correctly.	If you want to set up a trust yourself, there are books that show you how and computer programs that will generate one for you. If you decide to do it yourself, I urge you to have a qualified attorney look it over to make sure you did it correctly.
How much should it cost if an attorney creates one?	Depending on where you live and how complex your affairs are, a will should cost from around a hundred to a few hundred dollars.	Depending on the size of the estate and how expensive the attorney is, a simple trust should cost around $500 to $3,000. If you want your attorney to fund the trust—that is, transfer your assets into it—it may cost more.
What if I want to make a change?	When you want to change anything in the will, you simply draw up what is called a codicil, which is an additional paper enumerating your changes.	Once the trust is set up, making simple changes to it should cost about $100. Fees will vary depending on where you live and how complex your requirements are.
How many witnesses do I need?	Depending on the state you live in, you need to have either two or three people witness your signature on the will and sign it. To be on the safe side, ask three people to be witnesses.	Depending on the state you live in, you need to have either two or three people sign and witness your signature on a trust and sign the document. To be on the safe side, ask three people to be witnesses.

QUICK REFERENCE GUIDE:
A-B TAX PLANNING TRUST VERSUS REVOCABLE LIVING TRUST

	A-B TAX-PLANNING TRUST	**REVOCABLE LIVING TRUST**
What is the difference?	An A-B trust (also known as a tax-planning trust, a credit shelter trust, a marital trust, or a bypass trust) is a single trust that can eliminate federal taxes on estates valued over $1,000,000.	A revocable living trust protects your estate from the probate court process and probate fees. It does not shelter your estate from federal estate taxes.
How can it help my beneficiaries?	It essentially allows you to double the money you can leave your beneficiaries, other than your spouse, without incurring estate taxes. Otherwise your beneficiaries are limited to the unified credit exemption for the year of your death. Any amount inherited above that exemption will be subject to an estate-tax rate that begins at 37% and goes as high as 50%.	It will eliminate probate fees, help to transfer the legal titles to your assets as quickly as possible, and protect you if you become incapacitated. Again, please note: It will not help on any level with the estate taxes above the unified credit exemptions.
What is the unified credit exemption?	It is the amount that your beneficiaries can inherit without having to pay federal estate taxes:	It is the amount that your beneficiaries can inherit without having to pay federal estate taxes:

For Deaths Occurring In	Highest Estate Exemption	Highest Estate- and Gift-Tax Rate		For Deaths Occurring In	Highest Estate Exemption	Highest Estate- and Gift-Tax Rate
2002	$1,000,000	50%		2002	$1,000,000	50%
2003	1,000,000	49		2003	1,000,000	49
2004	1,500,000	48		2004	1,500,000	48
2005	1,500,000	47		2005	1,500,000	47
2006	2,000,000	46		2006	2,000,000	46
2007	2,000,000	45		2007	2,000,000	45
2008	2,000,000	45		2008	2,000,000	45
2009	3,500,000	45		2009	3,500,000	45

After 2010, estate taxes are repealed and top gift-tax rate will be the top individual income-tax rate, scheduled to be 35% with a unified credit of $1,000,000.

After 2010, estate taxes are repealed and top gift-tax rate will be the top individual income-tax rate, scheduled to be 35% with a unified credit of $1,000,000.

ESTATE TAX YOU WILL OWE WITHOUT AN A-B TRUST

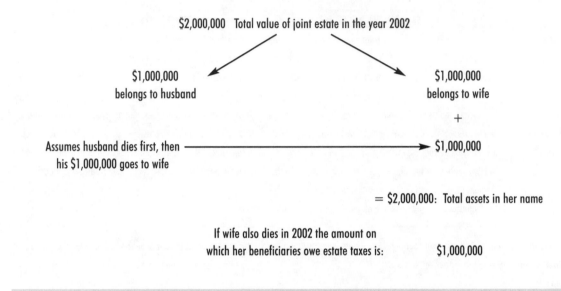

$2,000,000   Total value of joint estate in the year 2002

$1,000,000
belongs to husband

$1,000,000
belongs to wife

+

Assumes husband dies first, then
his $1,000,000 goes to wife $1,000,000

= $2,000,000: Total assets in her name

If wife also dies in 2002 the amount on
which her beneficiaries owe estate taxes is: $1,000,000

Assumes wife dies in 2002. The most she can leave her beneficiaries estate-tax free* is the unified exemption for 2002, $1,000,000. The estate tax is approximately 37%, or $370,000.

*Spouses can currently leave any amount of money to their spouse's estate tax-free upon their death, provided they are U.S. citizens.

HOW TO REDUCE ESTATE TAXES WITH AN A-B TRUST

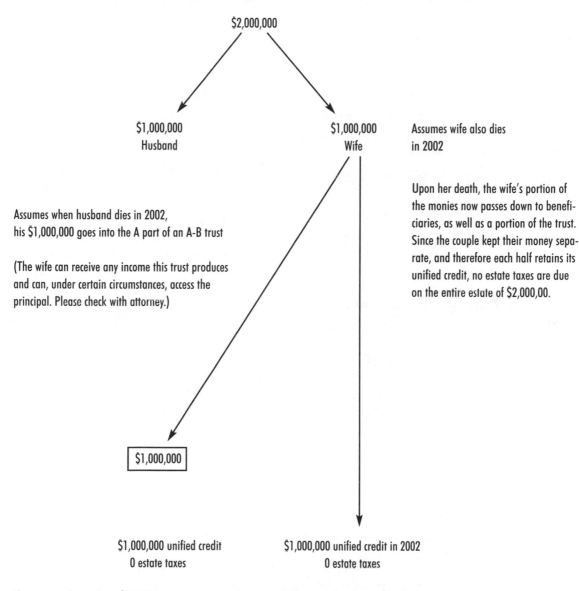

$2,000,000

$1,000,000
Husband

$1,000,000
Wife

Assumes wife also dies
in 2002

Assumes when husband dies in 2002,
his $1,000,000 goes into the A part of an A-B trust

(The wife can receive any income this trust produces
and can, under certain circumstances, access the
principal. Please check with attorney.)

Upon her death, the wife's portion of
the monies now passes down to beneficiaries, as well as a portion of the trust.
Since the couple kept their money separate, and therefore each half retains its
unified credit, no estate taxes are due
on the entire estate of $2,000,00.

$1,000,000

$1,000,000 unified credit
0 estate taxes

$1,000,000 unified credit in 2002
0 estate taxes

This just saved you about $370,000 in estate taxes in the year 2002 on an estate of up to $2,000,000.

QUICK REFERENCE GUIDE: TERMINOLOGY OF WILLS AND TRUSTS

TERM	DEFINITION	APPLIES TO WILL	TRUST
Administrator	The person who is appointed by the probate court, when there is no will, to collect assets of the estate, pay its debts, and distribute the rest to beneficiaries.	X	
Beneficiary	A person or organization designated to receive your assets upon your death.	X	X
Current beneficiaries	With a trust, the person or persons for whom all assets are being held in trust.		X
Estate	The sum total of all your financial interests, both money and property. Your estate is made up of everything you own at the time of your death, including life insurance, less your outstanding debts.	X	X
Executor	The person you appoint in your will to settle your estate. This person will have the administrative responsibility of paying your bills, dealing with the probate court, supervising the process of securing your assets, and making sure your wishes are carried out.	X	
Probate	A court procedure whereby (1) the judge authenticates a will and makes sure it is valid; (2) your executor or administrator is appointed; (3) your debts and taxes are paid; (4) your heirs are identified; and (5) property in your probate estate is distributed. Sounds simple, but in most states this process can take six months to two years and can be quite expensive.	X	
Remainder beneficiaries	With a trust, the person or persons who will inherit everything in the trust after the current beneficiary (who is usually the trustor as well) dies.		X
Successor trustee	The person who steps in to make decisions about the assets in a trust if and only if the trustee or co-trustees cannot or do not want to act in the decision-making process.		X
Testator	The person who creates a will.	X	
Trustor	The person who creates a trust and owns the property that will be put into the trust.		X
Trustee	The person or group of persons who controls the assets in the trust. Most often the trustor is also the trustee. When you set up a trust you do not have to give away your power over your assets. Most people continue taking care of everything just as they did before the trust existed.		X

ATTORNEY WORKSHEET

Company name: _____

Company phone number: _____

Company address: _____

Contact: _____

How long have you been specializing in estate planning? _____

How many people have you drafted wills and trusts for in the past five years? _____

Will you be drafting the documents yourself or will someone else be doing the paperwork? _____

How much do you charge? _____

If I have other questions, will you charge me if I call and ask? _____

Company name: _____

Company phone number: _____

Company address: _____

Contact: _____

How long have you been specializing in estate planning? _____

How many people have you drafted wills and trusts for in the past five years? _____

Will you be drafting the documents yourself or will someone else be doing the paperwork? _____

How much do you charge? _____

If I have other questions, will you charge me if I call and ask? _____

Company name: _____

Company phone number: _____

Company address: _____

Contact: _____

How long have you been specializing in estate planning? _____

How many people have you drafted wills and trusts for in the past five years? _____

Will you be drafting the documents yourself or will someone else be doing the paperwork? _____

How much do you charge? _____

If I have other questions, will you charge me if I call and ask? _____

PREPARING FOR YOUR INCAPACITY

Talking about wills and trusts, I've heard people say, "I don't care about any of this, because I am spending every penny I have while I am alive." In a way, I understand this. Once you die, money is not an issue anymore, is it?

But what if you don't die right away? What if you have a stroke or a skiing accident? What if you are incapacitated to the point where you are put on life support? What would you want to have happen then? If you do not decide now, someone else may decide for you later.

Most health insurance policies today have a maximum amount that they will pay out for an illness. This maximum varies from policy to policy, but the average is about $1 million. After your insurance company has paid out $1 million in benefits, it's done. With the cost of hospitalization skyrocketing, I am sure you can imagine that it would not take long to reach the maximum of your health insurance coverage if you happened to be on a life-support system in a hospital. Once the health insurance policy maximum has been reached, it is your loved ones who will be responsible for the medical bills that keep piling up. Having a durable power of attorney for health care is part of being responsible to your family, not only on an emotional level, but on a financial level as well.

For the sake of every one of you reading this guidebook, I hope that you won't ever be incapacitated or hospitalized, and that a long healthy life awaits you. But in case it doesn't, I urge you to make the simple arrangements for durable power of attorney for health care, for yourself and for the people you love. Do it now, while you're strong and healthy. It might be the most important document you ever sign. Most of the other subjects covered in this step concern your death. This one concerns your life.

Durable Power of Attorney for Health Care

What is a durable power of attorney for health care?

A durable power of attorney for health care is a document that enables you to put your feelings and wishes into effect regarding medical treatment and life support, and also specifies someone who will have the authority to make the decisions if you cannot do so because of an incapacity.

The first part of putting durable power of attorney for health care in place is deciding what you would want to have happen to you if you were incapacitated. It requires talking to your loved ones and making your feelings known. You can choose from three basic options.

1. You want to prolong your life for as long as possible, without regard to your condition, your chance of recovery, or the cost of treatment.

2. You want life-sustaining treatment to be provided unless you are in a coma or an ongoing vegetative state.

3. You do not want your life to be prolonged unnaturally, unless there is some hope that both your physical and mental health might be restored.

You must also decide in whose hands you want to put your life—who, that is, will make the final decision to take you off life support, if the decision ever has to be made. This person is known as the agent, and it is best to have two alternates, in case the person you have chosen is not available. Choose people who love you, yet who are strong enough to do what you would want them to do—this is not an easy position to be in.

I want you to take a moment to consider who you would want to be your agent and alternates for your durable power of attorney. This is one of the most important decisions you will make, so please do not rush into it. You do not need to decide at this moment. Give it careful thought, and when you have made up your mind, write their names below.

I will ask _____ to be my agent for my durable power of attorney for health care.

I will ask _____ to be an alternate agent for my durable power of attorney for health care.

I will ask _____ to be an alternate agent for my durable power of attorney for health care.

✓

Once you have decided whom you want to ask, get in touch with your chosen agent and alternates and find a time when you can discuss your decision with them in private. As difficult as this conversation may be, please do not put this step off. The moment you need this document, it's too late to create it.

The forms to establish durable power of attorney for health care vary from state to state but are available, free of charge, at every hospital. Just make sure you get the form that is valid in your state. You can also write to Partnership for Caring National Office, 1620 Eye Street NW, Suite 202, Washington, DC 20007, or call 800-989-WILL (9455), or visit the Web site www.partnershipforcaring.org to download forms. If you are using an attorney to create your trust or will, your attorney can take care of your durable power of attorney at the same time. Be sure to distribute copies to your doctor, agents, and alternate agents.

What is the difference between a living will and a durable power of attorney for health care?

A living will is not the same thing as a durable power of attorney and, in my opinion, is not as complete. A living will does make your wishes about life support known to the doctors, who then take them into consideration. It doesn't appoint someone you trust to make the final decision. A durable power of attorney for health care not only enables you to put your feelings and wishes into effect, but also specifies who will make the decision if you cannot. The living will, revocable living trust with incapacity clause, durable power of attorney, and durable power of attorney for health care are very different documents. The quick reference guide below gives an overview of the documents. Please note that you need both a revocable living trust with an incapacity clause and a durable power of attorney for health care.

QUICK REFERENCE GUIDE COMPARING INCAPACITY DOCUMENTS

	LIVING WILL OR DIRECTIVE TO PHYSICIANS	DURABLE POWER OF ATTORNEY FOR HEALTH CARE	DURABLE POWER OF ATTORNEY	REVOCABLE LIVING TRUST WITH INCAPACITY CLAUSE
What is the definition?	A document that advises your doctor of your desires regarding medical treatment and life support, but does not authorize anyone to make decisions for you. A living will cannot be changed significantly if your needs should change.	A document, created while you are still capable of expressing your desires regarding medical treatment and life support, that gives someone you designate the authority to make medical decisions for you if you are incapable of making them yourself.	A document that indicates that you have authorized someone to make legal and financial decisions on your behalf and that stays in effect even when you are incapacitated. A regular power of attorney becomes null and void when you are incapacitated.	A trust with a clause in which you name the person responsible for deciding when you are no longer capable of managing your own financial affairs.
How are they different?	A living will only advises your doctor of your desires regarding medical treatments and life support; it does not designate someone to make medical decisions for you or authorize someone to make legal or financial decisions for you.	A durable power of attorney for health care gives someone you designate the authority to make medical decisions for you—this is the only document that allows this to happen. It does not authorize anyone to make legal or financial decisions for you.	A durable power of attorney authorizes someone to make legal and financial decisions on your behalf but not medical decisions.	A revocable living trust with an incapacity clause gives someone the authority to make financial decisions but not medical decisions for you.
What will happen if I don't have one?	If you are incapacitated, your doctor will not be directly advised of your desires regarding medical treatments and life support.	If you end up in a hospital on life support and there's no hope of recovery, no one will be authorized to take you off life support. After your health insurance has been exhausted, you will have to use up your own and your family's assets to be kept alive, which could cost you everything you have saved.	You will need to be declared incompetent and have a conservatorship assigned to you (average cost is $5,000 and a judge would have to OK all decisions).	You will need to be declared incompetent and have a conservatorship assigned to you (average cost is $5,000 and a judge would have to OK all expenditures).
How do I get one?	Forms can be procured at most hospitals or public health services in your area. For more information or to obtain forms, contact Partnership for Caring at 800-989-WILL (9455) or visit its Web site, www.partnershipforcaring.org.	Forms can be procured at most hospitals or public health services in your area. For more information or to obtain forms, contact Partnership for Caring at 800-989-WILL (9455) or visit its Web site www.partnershipforcaring.org.	If you want to do it yourself, legal forms can be obtained from an office supply store, or there are computer programs that can generate one. Or you can get one from an attorney.	Include an incapacity clause when you are drafting your revocable living trust. You can create one with a book or computer program, but please have an attorney review it for you.

LIFE INSURANCE

So now you have all your documents in place, or you are aware of the documents that you need to get in place, to empower those you love when you're incapacitated or the day comes that you're no longer here. Many of us also like to provide financially for those we're going to leave behind. One of the main ways that we do this is by purchasing a life insurance policy. What's so interesting about this is that life insurance was never meant to be a permanent need. Its original purpose was to protect people while they were younger, before they had a chance to build up a nest egg, in case the family breadwinner died early and unexpectedly. If the breadwinner lived his or her life according to plan, however, the family would accumulate enough assets to make itself safe and let the insurance go.

Today, however, a huge industry exists to sell you as much insurance as it can, whether you really need it or not.

I know how the industry works, because I'm a licensed insurance agent, and I know the workings of most policies inside out. I also know how the commissions work. If you knew how large the commissions on life insurance policies such as whole-life policies really are—often 80 to 90 percent of the first year's premium—you would know why one of my favorite sayings is:

Life insurance is not something that is bought—
it is something that is sold to you.

Many people think of life insurance as a universal financial-planning tool, as a safe haven for savings and a substantial legacy for the family after they have gone. As we grow older, however, we find that there are often better places to hold—and grow—our money, and there can be serious disadvantages to leaving a large life insurance policy among our assets when we die. In any case, no one should ever use life insurance, or any kind of insurance, as a savings vehicle.

Who Can Skip This Section?

If you're single and have no dependents whatsoever, you can skip this section and go to page 73, because there is no need for you to have life insurance. If you have relatives who depend on the money you bring in with every paycheck, however, the following information is essential for you to understand.

Life Insurance Questions

How do I know if I or my life partner needs life insurance?

First you need to figure out how your income and expenses are going to change in the event that one of you should die. Here's how. On the worksheets below and on the next page, list how your family budget would be different if either you or your life partner were to die. Most of the household fixed expenses would be the same for the survivor, since you would still need to maintain your home (pay the mortgage, pay for gas and electricity, and pay for home insurance). Write the total amount for each of these expenses in both columns on the next page. Other categories of expenses (clothing, groceries, medical insurance, auto expenses, hair/manicure/facial, hobbies, etc.) might increase or decrease. Write the total of the yearly expenses at the bottom of the worksheet.

After you have compiled the information on your family expenses, take some time to figure out how your family's financial situation would change if your children were suddenly without one or both parents. What if the remaining partner had to go to work? Would your child-care situation change? If so, you need to add that expense. Could the remaining partner's income cover the financial goals you've set for the future—paying for your children's education, for example? How much do you have saved?

Now you need to figure out how much income you would have coming in if you or your life partner died. Fill in the worksheet below and total your yearly income as well as that of your life partner.

HOW A DEATH WOULD CHANGE MY FAMILY INCOME WORKSHEET		
	My Yearly Income	**My Life Partner's Yearly Income**
Yearly paychecks after taxes/deductions		
Predictable bonuses		
Social Security income		
Disability income		
Bond/interest income		
Interest income		
Dividend income		
Rental income		
Gifts from parents (if you can count on them)		
Loan repayments		
Pension income		
IRA income		
Miscellaneous		
TOTAL		

HOW A DEATH WOULD CHANGE MY FAMILY EXPENSES WORKSHEET

	My Yearly Expenses	My Life Partner's Yearly Expenses
Mortgage/rent		
Property taxes		
Home maintentance/condo fees		
Home insurance		
Gas & electric		
Water		
Garbage removal		
Telephone/cellular phone		
Burglar alarm		
House cleaner		
Gardening		
Pool/spa		
Firewood		
Food/restaurants		
Medical/dental/optometric		
Veterinarian		
Insurance		
Auto expenses		
Tolls/parking/transportation		
Clothes/shoes		
Dry cleaning		
Jewelry		
Hair/manicure/facial		
Alimony/child support		
Kids' school		
Job training/education		
Income taxes		
Legal/accounting fees		
Safe deposit box		
Computers		
Credit cards/loans		
Bank/credit union fees		
Express mail/postage		
Books/subscriptions		
Entertainment/video rentals		
Cable TV		
Sporting events		
Vacations		
Hobbies		
Donations		
Gifts		
Lottery		
Cigarettes		
Miscellaneous		
TOTAL		

Now it is time to figure out where your family would stand if you or your life partner were to die. How much would it really take to live? How much do you really have?

From the "How a Death Would Change My Family Income" worksheet on page 62, write your yearly income and your life partner/spouse's total yearly income in the box below.

From the "How a Death Would Change My Family Expenses" worksheet on page 63, write your yearly expenses and your life partner/spouse's total yearly expenses in the box below.

WHERE DO WE STAND IF THERE WAS A DEATH?

MY YEARLY INCOME $	MY LIFE PARTNER'S YEARLY INCOME $
minus (–)	minus (–)
MY YEARLY EXPENSES $	MY LIFE PARTNER'S YEARLY EXPENSES $
DIFFERENCE (yearly deficit or excess) $	DIFFERENCE (yearly deficit or excess) $

Now subtract your yearly expenses from your yearly income to determine your deficit or excess. Then subtract your life partner's yearly expenses from your life partner's yearly income to determine his or her deficit or excess.

Please answer yes or no to the following questions:

	YES	NO
Do either you or your life partner have a deficit?	____	____
If either you or your life partner died, would the survivor be unable to maintain the household expenses without going into debt?	____	____
If either you or your life partner died, would the survivor be unable to achieve your financial goals for your family?	____	____

If you answered no to all of the questions above, then you do not need life insurance. You may still want some for peace of mind, but you don't need it—and there is a big difference between needing it and wanting it.

If you answered yes to any of the questions above, then you do need life insurance to protect yourself and your loved ones.

✓

How much life insurance do I and my life partner need?

Most people think, "Oh, all I'd need is enough to get my family by for just a little while." As a result, they usually have $50,000 or so worth of insurance as part of their benefits package at work and feel that is more than enough. But since an unexpected tragedy affects different people in different ways, you never know for sure what might happen after you are gone. That's why this is a decision—taking into account every tragic possibility—that must be discussed with the people who would be affected by such an event. All the questions must be asked. Would they feel comfortable knowing that they have enough money to get by for a year, or two, or eight? Many experts will tell you to purchase six to eight times your annual salary, but experts are not the ones who will live your loved ones' lives. Maybe in your situation you would rather know that everyone will be OK no matter what, even if no one is ever able to work again. Maybe you want your children to be provided for for ten years, rather than just eight. There is no magic formula. Each person has his or her own financial what-if comfort level. The final decision is a balance of what makes everyone concerned feel secure—and how much you can realistically afford to pay for that security.

As a rule of thumb, I would figure on needing about $100,000 in insurance for every $500 of monthly income required, including income taxes. (A death benefit payment from the insurance company will not be taxed, but you are going to invest this money for income, and that income *will* be taxed.) Let's say your household needs $3,000 a month to cover all expenses and income taxes, and your worst-case scenario is that the people who survive will have no wages or other income, so they will need the full $3,000. You'd divide this by $500 and get six, so in this case your insurance policy should be six times $100,000, or $600,000 worth of insurance coverage.

Let's figure out how much projected monthly insurance income you or your life partner/spouse needs. In the box below write the deficit, from the chart "Where Do We Stand If There Was a Death" on page 64. Then divide that number by 12 to come up with the projected monthly insurance income needed.

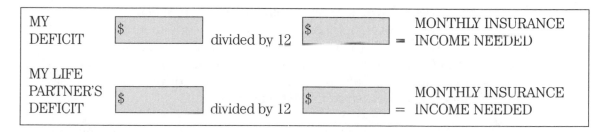

MY
DEFICIT $ _____ divided by 12 $ _____ MONTHLY INSURANCE
                                                        = INCOME NEEDED

MY LIFE
PARTNER'S
DEFICIT $ _____ divided by 12 $ _____ MONTHLY INSURANCE
                                                        = INCOME NEEDED

Now take the monthly insurance income needed and plug that number into the chart below to find out what the death benefit in your insurance policy should be.

	Income I need	Income my life partner needs
Projected monthly insurance income needed is A	A: _____	A: _____
Divide A by $500 to get B	B: _____	B: _____
Multiply B by $100,000 to get C	C: _____	C: _____

The amount of death benefit you need in an insurance policy is C.
Write the death benefit insurance amounts you and life partner need below.

I need a death benefit insurance of $ _____.

My life partner needs a death benefit insurance of $ _____.

This is the idea: You want your insurance payment to be the sum of money that your beneficiaries can invest to generate enough income to cover their expenses, including income taxes, without having to dip into principal. If their monthly expenses are $3,000, that is $36,000 a year. Assuming a conservative interest rate of 6 percent, you would need $600,000 to produce that $36,000 a year. The principal could continue to generate income indefinitely, as long as your survivors spent only the interest.

✓

How long will I and my life partner need life insurance?

That depends. Remember, life insurance was never intended to fill a permanent need. As the years go by, the money that you are putting away in your retirement plan, the money you may accumulate on your own, and the mortgage you're paying off to own your own home are all factors that will continue to change how much insurance you need, or whether you need any at all. One of the goals of this guidebook is to make sure that by the time you are retired, you'll have enough coming in from your retirement plans to support you and your loved ones, and to go on supporting them after you're gone. Once you have saved enough to live on, there will probably be no need for life insurance. (However, never, never cancel or attempt to change a policy without checking with your doctor and having a thorough physical. If there's a medical reason, you may want to keep insurance you otherwise would not have needed.)

Bottom-line goal: By the time you are retired, your need for life insurance and your need to pay the premiums on your life insurance should be gone. If you have children, you may carry life insurance to provide for them into early adulthood. If so, you may want to consider insurance until your youngest child is twenty-four. By that time your children should be able to take care of themselves if something unexpected were to happen to you.

So please ask yourself, how many years will you and your life partner need life insurance? Please write the number of years in the spaces below:

I will need life insurance _____ years.

My life partner will need life insurance _____ years.

✓

What kind of life insurance do I or my life partner need?

In my opinion, there is only one kind of life insurance that makes sense for the vast majority of us, and that is term life insurance. When you sign up for term insurance, you're buying a just-in-case policy for the finite length of time for which you need protection. Term policies are not very expensive, because the insurance company knows you have relatively little chance of dying while the policy is in force. Most likely the company won't have to pay a death benefit, and accordingly the premium is relatively small.

With a whole-life or universal policy, on the other hand, you are buying the policy with the intention of keeping it for your "whole life," and so the insurance company knows it will almost certainly have to pay the face amount, or the death benefit. You're expected to die with it. So the company prices it accordingly. It's true that whole life and universal policies have cash values, and if you decide not to keep your policy, or if you suddenly need money, you could tap into the cash value of the policy. But commissions on life insurance policies are some of the most lucrative commissions in any business—and you're paying them. If your goal in buying life insurance is to put money aside, there are far, far better ways to save it without having to pay commissions like these, as we'll see in the next steps. With low-cost term insurance, even though you do not accumulate a cash value, you're paying a low commission on the protection you need, for as long as you signed up for.

QUICK REFERENCE GUIDE:
TERM LIFE INSURANCE VERSUS WHOLE-LIFE INSURANCE

	TERM LIFE INSURANCE	**WHOLE-LIFE INSURANCE**
How are they different?	Term life Insurance is good for only a specific period of time. The terms that you can choose vary from one to five to ten to twenty years.	Whole-life insurance is designed to remain in force regardless of how long you live.
What is the difference in cost?	Term insurance is by far the most cost-effective life insurance that you can buy and is considerably less expensive than any other kind. Your annual premium is based upon the length of the term that you choose, along with your age and health at the time you apply for coverage. For example, if you are a healthy forty-year-old man who doesn't smoke, a twenty-year term life policy with a $300,000 death benefit would cost you about $42 a month.	Whole-life insurance is far more expensive because the insurer will pay out a death benefit if your policy is in force when you die. Please keep in mind that insurance companies calculate their premiums so that they tend to make at least that amount and more on the money you pay in over the years. For example, if you were a healthy forty-year-old man who doesn't smoke, a whole-life policy with a $300,000 death benefit would cost you about $338.64 a month.
What if I decide not to keep it or not to renew?	Term insurance has no cash value if you decide to cancel your policy. For those who do renew their policies when the term runs out, the policy in most circumstances can be replaced but it will be priced according to your age, health, and the term at time of renewal. The older you are, the greater the cost because, actuarially speaking, you are closer to your probable age of death. The cost to renew a term policy for someone in his or her seventies or eighties would very likely be prohibitive.	A whole-life policy has cash value, so if you decide not to keep it, or if you suddenly need money while you are alive, one source would be the cash value of the policy. But buyer beware: Commissions on life insurance policies are some of the most lucrative commissions in any business, so you could find that the cash value of your insurance is far less than you expected.

Short-Term? Long-Term?

Term insurance is available in various term lengths, from yearly renewable term, where every year your premium will go up, to level term for longer terms—five, seven, ten, fifteen years, and so on—where the premium is fixed for the term. So when you buy term insurance, you will need to get quotes on both renewable term and level term.

If I have whole-life insurance, what do I do?

First, you should go to a doctor and make sure that you have a clean bill of health. Then you can apply for and purchase a term life insurance policy for whatever length of time you think you require it in order to put enough money in savings and retirement accounts to provide for your family if you die. Once you have been approved for your new term policy, then and only then should you cash out your whole-life policy and invest the "cash value" in a good no-load mutual fund. Add to your mutual fund what you're saving on premiums, which will be much lower with term than with whole life.

I told my insurance agent that I wanted to cash out of my whole-life policy. He says if I cash out now I'll be losing money. Is that true?

You may be losing some of your investment in the short term because the insurance company has deducted so much in fees, but you are almost certainly going to make it up and then some over the long run (ten or more years) if you invest that cash value and the excess premium money in a no-load mutual fund. The insurance company is the party that is really going to lose money, because it will not have the use of yours anymore.

Is it ever a good idea to take out a life insurance policy on another person?

It can be a good idea, if you have a financial interest in that person—usually a life partner or a business partner. But please do not take out life insurance policies on your small children. Remember, life insurance is meant to replace income that other people are dependent on. Your small child has no income and doesn't need her own life insurance. She needs your life insurance, if something should happen to you.

Summarize Your Life Insurance Needs

Please answer the questions below to see if you or your life partner needs life insurance and, if so, how much and for how long.

MY LIFE INSURANCE SUMMARY

Do I need it? (page 62)	Yes _____ No _____
How much do I need? (page 65)	_____
How long will I need it? (page 66)	_____
What kind of insurance policy do I need?	_____ TERM _____

MY LIFE PARTNER'S LIFE INSURANCE SUMMARY

Do I need it? (page 62)	Yes _____ No _____
How much do I need? (page 65)	_____
How long will I need it? (page 66)	_____
What kind of insurance policy do I need?	_____ TERM _____

✓

If You Need Life Insurance

Please use one of the quoting services listed below and be prepared to provide the following information: sex, date of birth, health (current health as well as medical history of the applicant), how much insurance, and for how long it is needed.

AccuQuote	(800) 442-9899	www.accuquote.com
DirectQuote	(800) 845-3853	www.directquote.com
Insurance Quote Services	(800) 972-1104	www.iquote.com
InsWeb	(800) 871-5075	www.insweb.com
LifeRates of America	(800) 457-2837	
MasterQuote	(800) 337-5433	www.masterquote.com
Quotesmith	(800) 556-9393	www.quotesmith.com
Select Quote	(800) 343-1985	www.selectquote.com
TermQuote	(800) 444-8376	www.termquote.com

Spend an hour this weekend checking out the quoting services just listed. If you already have insurance, use these services to compare prices to see if you can get a better deal. Also check with at least three of the rating services listed on the next page; you may be surprised to see how much they can differ. Please use the quote worksheet on page 72 to assist you in keeping track of the information.

How should you choose your insurance policy? Which is the best one to go with?

Don't Purchase Term Insurance Strictly on the Basis of Price

The cheapest policy will not always be the best one for you, because you're not just comparing costs—you are also comparing resources and services. Insist that the insurance company send you—in writing—its rating from at least two of the independent insurance rating services listed below. Or call the rating companies yourself to check the current ratings of insurance companies you are interested in buying from. The rating you are looking for is either A+ or better or AA or better.

A.M. Best	(908) 439-2200	A+ or better
Duff & Phelps	(312) 263-2610	AA or better
Moody's	(212) 553-0377	AA or better
Standard & Poor's	(212) 438-2000	AA or better

Review Your Policies Yearly

Make sure that your policies are still exactly corresponding to your needs. Each year, ask yourself the following questions:

	YES	NO
Did I make major improvements to my house?	_____	_____
Did my youngest child finish college?	_____	_____
Did my spouse become eligible for Social Security?	_____	_____
Has my expected income increased or decreased substantially?	_____	_____
Have I had an addition to my family (marriage, birth of a child, adoption)?	_____	_____
Has a death occurred that affects my household income?	_____	_____

If you answered yes to any of these questions on life changes, you should look over your insurance policy because you may need to change your coverage.

✓

INSURANCE QUOTE WORKSHEET

Quoting service #1: _____

Company phone number: _____

Company address: _____

Contact: _____

Length of term: _____

Death benefit: _____

Cost of premium: _____

Insurer: _____

Rating: _____

Quoting service #2: _____

Company phone number: _____

Company address: _____

Contact: _____

Length of term: _____

Death benefit: _____

Cost of premium: _____

Insurer: _____

Rating: _____

Quoting service #3: _____

Company phone number: _____

Company address: _____

Contact: _____

Length of term: _____

Death benefit: _____

Cost of premium: _____

Insurer: _____

Rating: _____

✓

LONG-TERM-CARE INSURANCE

Of all the kinds of insurance available out there, long-term-care (LTC) insurance is the one that people seem most resistant to purchasing. Oddly enough, it's the one that most of you will probably need. If you own a home you have fire insurance, yet only one out of 1,200 of you will ever use it. All of you who own a car have car insurance, yet only 1 out of 240 of you will ever use it. But 1 out of 3 of you will wish you had owned long-term-care insurance, because 1 out of 3 of you will spend some time in a nursing home after age sixty-five. LTC insurance is used more than any other kind of insurance, yet it's the kind of policy that way too few of us have.

Your health insurance will not pay for long-term-care. There is not one health insurance policy in existence that covers this kind of care. Medicare in most cases will not pay for it, or if it does pay, it will pay the full cost of a nursing home stay for only twenty days and part of the cost for only another eighty days, after which you are on your own. Medicaid will pay for it, but only if you are financially destitute.

There is nothing we can do about catastrophic or chronic illness if and when it hits, but we can take the steps today to help make sure that our loved ones' tomorrows are protected financially.

Why Is Long-Term-Care Insurance a Bargain for Many of Us?

In my opinion, the best time to purchase an LTC policy is at around age fifty-nine, although this insurance can be a bargain at any price if you're older. Regardless of your age, if you do have to go into a nursing home one day, you will almost certainly pay less for all your payments on an LTC policy than you would for one year in the nursing home. And many people live in nursing homes much longer than one year. The average length of stay is 2.9 years, or 8.0 years for people with Alzheimer's disease.

LTC premiums are based on how old you are when you purchase the policy and are projected to remain stable for the lifetime of the policy. Once you need to use the policy, all premium payments will be waived; from that point on it is free as long as you are using the benefits. This is not one of those policies where you will outsmart the insurance company by waiting to buy it. It doesn't work like that. Rule of thumb: The longer you wait, the more it will cost.

Good nursing home care in the year 2002 costs about $4,500 per month in some areas, and in major cities some of the most pleasant nursing homes are already $9,000 a month. That's what it costs today—who knows what it will cost in your particular location ten, twenty, thirty, forty years from now? You cannot afford to wait to find out.

How Can I Tell If I Can Afford Long-Term-Care Insurance?

If you are not able to pay your bills or are just making ends meet each month, long-term-care insurance is certainly not for you. But if you are able to save some of your income each month after expenses, you have liquid assets of at least $50,000, and you own your home, then long-term-care insurance may be worth your while. The key thing is to be absolutely sure that you will be able to continue to pay the premiums once you are retired.

Ask yourself the following questions:

Could I keep paying for this policy if my yearly premiums increased by 20 percent?

If my income decreases in the future, will I be able to pay the yearly premiums easily?

If you answered no to these questions, LTC insurance is most likely not for you.

Long-term-care insurance is meant to keep you from going into the poorhouse due to a long-term-care stay in a nursing home, not put you in the poorhouse to pay for it. You have to be able to afford the premiums both now and in the years after you retire. It will do you no good to buy a policy at fifty-nine, retire at sixty-four, and find, at seventy-four, that you can no longer afford the premiums. No matter how long you've paid into an annual-premium policy, once you stop paying you'll no longer be covered. You would have been better off not purchasing the insurance in the first place and investing the money instead.

If you can't afford LTC insurance, you can still be responsible to those you love. If you are worried about your aging parents or, when the time comes, about yourself, you can seek out the advice of an attorney who specializes in elder care. If your parents live far away, see an elder-care attorney near where they live, not where you live, because the assistance available varies widely from state to state and can even vary from region to region within the same state. In any case, an elder-care attorney will go over all the options available to you—and these keep changing.

If you can afford it, LTC insurance is in my opinion the most useful insurance you will ever have. The key, however, is buying the correct coverage for the correct price with the right insurance company.

How Do I Choose a Long-Term-Care Insurance Company?

When I first started researching long-term-care insurance in 1986, there were only about four companies selling it. Today there are more than 100, and that number generally fluctuates by 30 or 40, depending on which companies have decided to give it a try and which have decided to check out of the LTC business. When you buy your LTC insurance, you won't plan on using it for many years, if ever. But it is important that the company you buy the policy from will still be there if ever you need it.

Here are some companies with a track record that you may want to consider:

General Electric Capital Assurance Company	(800) 844-6543 or (800) THINK GE	www.gefn.com
CNA (Continental Casualty)	(800) 775-1541	www.cna.com
John Hancock	(800) 732-5543	www.jhancock.com
UNUM Provident	(800) 227-8138	www.unumprovident.com

Essential Questions

Questions about the Provider

Here are the questions you must ask each company you are considering, and the acceptable answers. These are good questions to ask when considering buying any policy, but essential in the case of long-term care.

How long have you been selling LTC insurance?

The only acceptable answer is ten years, minimum. If the answer is one year, two years,or three years, the company is still experimenting.

How much LTC insurance do you currently have in force?

The only acceptable answer is hundreds of millions of dollars. With that much money in LTC insurance, the company is already making a handsome profit—and not thinking of getting out of the business.

How many times have you had a rate increase for those who already own a policy?

The only acceptable answer is two times or fewer. The "already own a policy" phrase is important. You are not looking at rate increases for people who have not yet purchased a policy. You are looking at rate increases for people who have already taken the plunge, bought the insurance, and are therefore vulnerable to the whims of the insurance company.

In how many states are you currently selling LTC insurance?

The only acceptable answer is every state. If the company is selling LTC insurance in only one state—yours—you can be sure it is still experimenting.

Is your company—or its LTC division—on the block to be sold?

The answer you want to hear is no. Even if the company has a great LTC track record now, you don't know the track record or commitment to LTC of the company that will purchase it.

What are the ratings from the independent services? (These services rate the safety and soundness of insurance carriers.)

To save some time, please refer to the insurance rating services listed on page 71. Check with at least three of these services; you may be surprised how much they can differ.

At least two of the rating services listed must have awarded the insurance company their ratings of A+ or AA or better. Insist that the insurance company send you their ratings in writing, or call the rating services yourself.

Questions about the Policy

Here are the questions you need to keep in mind when inquiring about the policy itself. Use the worksheet on page 79 to record the information.

What does it take to qualify for benefits?

In order for you to qualify for benefits and have your insurance company start paying your LTC bills, you are going to have to prove to the company that you really do, in fact, need long-term care. This is called making it through the gatekeepers. You won't see a penny until you qualify for benefits.

If you have a tax-qualified plan—which is quickly becoming the most common type of plan—the only acceptable answer to the question of how you qualify for benefits is meeting either one of the two conditions that follow.

The first gatekeeper is not to be able to carry out certain *activities of daily living (ADLs).* In order to function normally, most of us need to be able to 1) feed ourselves; 2) clothe ourselves; 3) transfer ourselves (get in and out of bed, chairs, and the like, unattended); 4) be continent; 5) use the toilet; and 6) bathe ourselves (California only). With a good policy, if you got to a point in your life where you could not perform *any two* of the qualifying ADLs in your state, then you would qualify for benefits.

The second gatekeeper is *cognitive impairment,* which simply means that you qualify if you come down with, say, Alzheimer's disease or cannot think or act clearly and therefore cannot care for yourself.

By the way, don't be surprised if you run into two types of plans: tax-qualified (like the above) and what's called non-tax-qualified. An important note here is that with a tax-qualified plan (TQ), your LTC insurance premiums may be tax-deductible as a medical expense, if your premiums, along with other deductible out-of-pocket medical expenses, come to 7.5 percent of your adjusted gross income. A non-tax-qualified plan (NTQ), which has become less common in recent years, doesn't offer you the possible tax deduction but *does* let you claim your benefits with one other gatekeeper, which is known as *medical necessity;* this is where a doctor states that it is medically necessary for you to have long-term care; for example, if you are unstable and in danger of falling.

In the past, I have always liked NTQ policies more than TQ policies. That said, today many insurance companies are no longer even offering NTQ plans. The government has stated the possibility that the benefits you might one day receive in your NTQ plan could be taxed; so if you ever use the benefits, you might have to pay taxes on them (although most likely you would have at least a partial offset for deductible medical expenses). Therefore, our choices are becoming more limited, with the result that a tax-qualified plan is probably the way we have to go.

To find out more about the differences, you can call the Health Insurance Counseling and Advocacy Program (800-434-0222) to find an office near you that can provide more information.

How much should I spend on long-term-care insurance?

You should spend no more than 5 to 7 percent of your monthly income on premiums. This is the type of insurance where it really pays to compare prices, because policies vary significantly in terms of the benefits they offer.

How much should a long-term-care insurance policy cost me?

If you find the right company, you may not have to pay as much as you think you will. Assuming that you are in excellent health, the example on the next page shows what an excellent long-term-care policy from a good company with a $130 daily benefit amount (the current average nationwide), six-year coverage, no (or not more than 60 days) elimination period, a compounded 5 percent inflation provision, survivorship benefit, and full nursing-home and home-care coverage might cost you in 2002, depending on your age.

Here is an example of long-term-care annual premiums:

Age	Cost
40–45	$1,596
46	1,634
47	1,660
48	1,686
49	1,699
50	1,725
51	1,763
52	1,828
53	1,879
54	1,956
55	2,033
56	2,136
57	2,265
58	2,394
59	2,561
60	2,728
61	2,921
62	3,102
63	3,320
64	3,539
65	3,758
66	4,015
67	4,311
68	4,710
69	5,135
70	5,611

Please note: The daily benefit amount, the benefit period, the inflation provision, and the home-health-care coverage will all need to be identical when you are comparing prices among different companies. There can be big pricing differences among companies offering LTC insurance (or any insurance, for that matter). I have seen policies from two or three carriers offering essentially the same benefits with a difference of up to $1,500 a year. When you compare prices, make sure that you are comparing apples with apples—comparing exactly the same benefits across the board. Otherwise the price comparisons won't yield the information you're looking for.

LONG-TERM-CARE INSURANCE WORKSHEET

Insurance company #1: _____

Company phone number: _____

Company address: _____

Contact: _____

What is the daily benefit? _____

What is the benefit period? _____

What is the elimination period? _____

What is the inflation rider? _____

What is the home-health-care clause? _____

Qualification of benefits: Medical necessity _____   Impairment in ADLs _____   Cognitive impairment _____

Cost of yearly premium? _____

How long selling LTC? _____

How much LTC do you have in force? _____

How many times has the rate increased for those who already own a policy? _____

In how many states are you currently selling LTC? _____

Is your company on the block to be sold? _____

How are you rated? _____

Insurance company #2: _____

Company phone number: _____

Company address: _____

Contact: _____

What is the daily benefit? _____

What is the benefit period? _____

What is the elimination period? _____

What is the inflation rider? _____

What is the home-health-care clause? _____

Qualification of benefits: Medical necessity _____   Impairment in ADLs _____   Cognitive impairment _____

Cost of yearly premium? _____

How long selling LTC? _____

How much LTC do you have in force? _____

How many times has the rate increased for those who already own a policy? _____

In how many states are you currently selling LTC? _____

Is your company on the block to be sold? _____

How are you rated? _____

✓

With long-term-care insurance in place, you will have gone a long, long way toward being responsible not only to those you love, but also to yourself and the money you've worked so hard to earn.

LONG-TERM-DISABILITY INSURANCE

Long-term-disability (LTD) insurance is another kind of insurance that can protect you if a catastrophe prevents you from being able to earn a living. Depending on the kind of work you do, an injury, an illness, or certain chronic conditions could cut off your income for a long time or even permanently. Disability policies will usually pay 60 to 70 percent of your current salary in the event of such a disability.

Suppose you do heavy labor and are laid up with a back injury, or you are a psychotherapist and lose your ability to speak because of a stroke. When this kind of disaster strikes, an LTD policy can save the day. You may think that you do not need one because you are protected by workers' compensation. Remember that workers' compensation covers you only if you are injured while performing your job. LTD insurance will pay whether you hurt yourself on the job or at home or on vacation.

In many ways this insurance is every bit as complicated in terms of finding a good policy as long-term-care insurance is.

Essential Questions

Questions about the Provider

Please refer to page 75 for the essential questions you should ask a long-term-care provider. These are the same questions you should ask a long-term-disability provider.

Questions about the Policy

In looking for a good policy, here are some elements that you need to understand and some further information to seek.

What percentage of income will the policy pay?

Most policies pay a percentage of what you are earning; typically they range from 60 to 90 percent of your current salary. The higher the percentage, the more expensive the policy usually is. With employer-provided policies, many companies have a cap on how much they will pay monthly; for large employers it is usually $5,000 a month.

How long is my elimination period, or waiting period?

Just as with LTC policies, this is how long you will have to wait until the company starts to pay. A normal waiting period is three to six months.

Until what age will the policy pay?

Most policies pay only until you are sixty-five years of age.

Will the policy cover me if I am disabled because of illness as well as because of an accident?

The answer should be yes.

What if I can only work part-time because of my disability?

You want a policy that will pay according to how much you can and cannot work. So if you can work only part-time, the policy should pay a portion of your disability payments. The term for this is "residual benefits."

Should the policy be "owner's OCC" or "any OCC"?

This question is very important. What it asks is whether the company will pay you only if you cannot perform any job whatsoever, or will also pay if you cannot perform *your* job. Suppose you were a musician and you lost some of your hearing. You might be able to function and sell pencils on the street corner, so you would not necessarily be "disabled," but you wouldn't be able to do your job. If you had an "any OCC" disability policy, it would pay you only if you could not perform *any* occupation, so you would not be able to collect benefits as a result of your loss of hearing. If your policy was "owner OCC," it would pay as long as you, the policy owner, could not perform your own occupation.

Pricing

LTD insurance is even more expensive than LTC insurance, so it pays to shop around. The most cost-effective way to buy it is (usually) through your employer, if the employer offers it. In many states it is mandatory that your employer offer it to you in your benefits package, so depending on where you live you may already be covered. Make sure you ask your benefits person to find out if you are covered and, if so, how much coverage you have and how it works. If you do not feel that it is enough, or you are not covered, you might consider looking into purchasing some on your own.

The main companies that specialize in disability insurance are:

CNA (Continental Casualty)	(800) 775-1541	www.cna.com
Northwestern Mutual Life	(414) 271-1444	www.northwesternmutual.com
UNUM Provident	(800) 227-8138	www.unumprovident.com
USAA	(800) 531-8000	www.usaa.com

Please use the worksheet on the next page to assist you in keeping track of the different quotes.

LONG-TERM-DISABILITY INSURANCE WORKSHEET

Insurance company #1 _____

Company phone number _____

Company address _____

Contact _____

Cost of yearly premium _____

How long selling LTD? _____

How much LTD do you have in force? _____

How many times has the rate increased for those who already own a policy? _____

In how many states are you currently selling LTD? _____

Is your company on the block to be sold? _____

How are you rated? _____

What percentage of income will the policy pay? _____

How long is my elimination or waiting period? _____

Until what age will the policy pay? _____

Do you cover me if I am disabled because of illness as well as in an accident? _____

What if I can work only part-time because of my disability? _____

Is it "owner's OCC" or "any OCC"? _____

Insurance company #2 _____

Company phone number _____

Company address _____

Contact _____

Cost of yearly premium _____

How long selling LTD? _____

How much LTD do you have in force? _____

How many times has the rate increased for those who already own a policy? _____

In how many states are you currently selling LTD? _____

Is your company on the block to be sold? _____

How are you rated? _____

What percentage of income will the policy pay? _____

How long is my elimination or waiting period? _____

Until what age will the policy pay? _____

Do you cover me if I am disabled because of illness as well as in an accident? _____

What if I can work only part-time because of my disability? _____

Is it "owner's OCC" or "any OCC"? _____

✓

REVIEW

Please take the actions outlined in this step. Do one action this week—make a call, get quotes for insurance, ask your parents about what would happen if they had to go into a nursing home. One action this week will clear the way for you to take one action next week, and so on until you have become responsible to those you love.

STEP 5

Being Respectful of Yourself and Your Money

If you're respectful of your money and do what needs to be done with it, you will become like a magnet, attracting more and more money to yourself. This is one of the reasons why the rich get richer.

If you treat your money with disrespect, you are actually denying *yourself* the respect that you deserve. And when you fail to respect yourself and your money, you repel wealth from you and block more money from coming your way.

The consequences of not respecting money may show up in your life in any number of ways. You might lose some of what you have just because you've failed to pay attention. As soon as you pay off a credit card, your car breaks down; now you owe even more. Maybe you don't get the job you felt certain was yours. A wonderful relationship, or so you thought, goes out the window over money. However this repulsion takes place in your life, the root cause of it is disrespect of yourself and your money.

When I say this to people, some of them get very defensive and say, "But Suze, I am the most respectful person I know when it comes to money." When we look closely at all their actions relating to their money, however, we see that they are not as respectful as they would like to think.

When you start really respecting yourself, those you love, and your money, the result is that you start having control over your money. What follows from that is control over your life.

ARE YOU REPELLING MONEY? EXERCISE

Are you repelling money—preventing it from flowing in your direction? Consider the following examples to help you determine how you treat yourself and your money. Check yes or no.

	YES	NO
Do you spend more money on your friends than you can afford to?	_____	_____
Do you find yourself buying more birthday or holiday presents for your children than feels right to you?	_____	_____
Will you spend money on others but never a penny on yourself?	_____	_____
Do you send things Federal Express or next-day air because the service will come pick them up, instead of going to the post office to mail them far more cheaply?	_____	_____
Have you ever bought a sweater and decided, when you got it home, that it really didn't suit you, then failed to return it to the store in time to get your money back?	_____	_____
Do you borrow things from friends and not return them?	_____	_____
Do you sometimes "forget" to pay off personal loans from friends with the same regularity that you'd pay off a credit card debt?	_____	_____
Do you often return videos a day late and have to pay the late fee, even though you've already watched them?	_____	_____
Do you send your clothes out for dry cleaning when all they need is a quick once-over with an iron?	_____	_____
Do you often go out to dinner simply because you don't feel like cooking?	_____	_____
Do you sometimes pay your bills late when you don't have to?	_____	_____

If you checked yes more often than no, you are being disrespectful of yourself and your money.

Please write down all the ways in which you are both respectful and disrespectful of yourself and your money. Contemplate this for a while, and you'll begin to see how the actions you take can erode your relationship with yourself and with your money.

How are you respectful of yourself and your money? Please write your response below.

_____

_____

_____

_____

_____

_____

_____

_____

_____

_____

_____

_____

How are you disrespectful of yourself and your money? Please write your response below.

_____

_____

_____

_____

_____

_____

_____

_____

_____

_____

_____

_____

Go back and think about occasions when your respect led to something great happening. Write the highlights in the box below.

Has there been an incident when your disrespect brought with it some unhappy consequences? Describe it in the box below.

It's very subtle, but the way we treat ourselves and our money touches upon every aspect of our lives.

People who are respectful of themselves, respectful of others who have money as well as those who do not, and respectful of what money can and cannot do are said to have a golden touch. I'm sure you've said it yourself about someone: Whatever she touches turns to gold. But a golden touch with money isn't something you're born with, like perfect pitch in singing. It is something you can learn, something you *must* learn if you want to be blessed with Financial Freedom.

WALLET EXERCISE EXAM

Please take out your wallet or whatever you keep your money in right now. Look closely at the contents of your wallet and answer the following questions:

	YES	NO
Are the ones mixed in with the tens?	____	____
Are the bills all facing different ways?	____	____
Are they stuffed in there in such a way that you have to uncrumple them to see what they are?	____	____

✓

If you checked yes more often than no, you are being disrespectful of yourself and your money. How you keep your money is where respect for it starts.

WALLET CHECKLIST

Every morning before you leave the house I want you to look in your wallet and go through the actions shown on the following checklist.

_____ Arrange the bills in order, from one dollar bills on up.

_____ Have all the bills face the same way.

_____ Make sure the bills are all nice and crisp (if not, exchange them for crisp bills).

✓

By keeping your bills neat and in order, caring for them the way you care for other important things in your life, you will constantly remind yourself of the respect you and your money deserve. This is what Step 5 of the 9 Steps to Financial Freedom is about: being respectful of yourself and your money and taking actions to give that respect meaning.

DEBT

Your money is affected by how you treat it—it's that simple. It thrives when you are being responsible and respectful and doing honorable things with it. It tends to disappear when you treat it disrespectfully. For many of you, debt is too big a part of your overall financial picture not to give it the respect due. How you treat debt and the people who are a part of that debt plays a major role in your path to Financial Freedom.

Good Debt Versus Bad Debt

There is good debt and there is bad debt. Good debt is an investment in *you*. And there is nobody that I know you should invest in more than you. An example of good debt is a student loan. When you pay off a student loan, it makes you feel more powerful, and that helps you go out into the world to get the job that you deserve. Credit card debt is bad debt. For most of you, credit card debt is debt that you acquired because you wanted to fulfill present-day desires at the cost of your future needs. There is nothing more disrespectful of yourself and your peace of mind than having credit card debt.

Do You Have Shame about Credit Card Debt?

Please check yes or no.

	YES	NO
Do you hide the fact that you have credit card debt from your friends?	____	____
Are you ashamed of the fact that you have it?	____	____
When asked, do you pretend that you don't have any credit card debt?	____	____
When you go out to eat with your friends, do you offer to pay the entire bill and use your credit card to do so, even though you are struggling with credit card debt?	____	____
		✓

If you answered yes to any of these questions, not only do you have credit card debt but you have fear and shame about your debt.

Having credit card debt does not make you a bad person. Please know that you are worth far more than the negative balance on your credit card statements.

Debt of Any Kind Is Bondage

Debt can feel like the heaviest burden in life. It can weigh down your spirits, occupy your mind, and make you feel bound—because you are bound. When debt takes on a life of its own and grows faster than you can pay it, the weight of the debt displaces everything—the money you are saving for your future, your capacity to save and invest, your ability to pay off the debt as it keeps growing.

Facing Your Debt

As a crucial part of respecting yourself and your money, you must respect those to whom you *owe* money.

In this context, there are two kinds of debt:

Personal—to a friend, relative, or other person who has loaned you money
Institutional—to credit card companies, a bank, the IRS, schools, etc.

Whether you have personal or institutional debt, or both, you must face the debt head-on. Otherwise the disrespect starts to take root in your soul. Not paying your debts is a serious form of disrespect and makes it almost impossible to find new ways to create new money. Not paying debts will not make them go away; instead, it will make your money vanish, and possibly your friendships, too. Remember: *Disrespect repels money.*

ACTIONS TO RID YOURSELF OF DEBT FOREVER

Action 1: Determine How Much Debt You Have

The first action you need to take is determining how much debt you have. Please gather all of your statements. I'm going to ask you to face what you owe, and see what your creditors are charging you to owe it. Fill out the worksheet below, listing the debts with the highest interest rates first. Remember to include all your debts, including personal loans from family members, car loans, student loans, and home mortgage.

CREDITOR	BALANCE OWED	INTEREST RATE	MINIMUM PAYMENT	ACCOUNT NUMBER	SINGLE OR DOUBLE BILLING CYCLE*	PHONE NUMBER

*The billing cycle is the manner in which your creditors compute interest. This information is supplied on the back of your credit card statement. Get rid of any cards that have two-cycle average daily balances (see the question "How do you charge interest?" page 94).

Action 2: Tell a Trusted Friend

If you have been hiding the fact that you are in debt, the second action you need to take is telling a trusted friend. Tell him or her not only that you have debt, but how much debt you have.

Please do not be surprised when your friend admits that he or she has as much debt as you do, or more debt.

Action 3: Call Your Creditors and Get a Lower Interest Rate

Interest rates do make a difference.

Take a look at the table that follows. You will see how much more and how much longer you will pay when your interest rates are higher.

TIME AND INTEREST TO PAY OFF A $4,000 CREDIT CARD BALANCE

At This Interest Rate	Paying $100 Every Month, It Will Take You This Long to Pay	And You'll Pay This Much in Interest
5.9%	45 months	$ 465
7.9	47 months	648
9.9	49 months	874
12.9	53 months	1,257
15.9	58 months	1,736
18.9	63 months	2,362

Throwing away hundreds of dollars in unnecessary interest payments every year is truly being disrespectful of your money. If you cannot pay off the balance on your credit card, switch it to a card with a lower interest rate. Credit card companies want your business, and if you're a heavy user with a good credit history, they will make it easy for you to switch to the card they're offering. You can usually switch your balance to a lower (much lower) interest rate card with a few phone calls and five minutes of paperwork. Keep in mind that too-good-to-be-true offers are usually just that: too good to be true. Open and read every credit card offer you receive in the mail. It may be that you have to roll over your debt two or three times a year to get the best deals. That's a few calls and fifteen minutes of paperwork a year, and it could save you literally hundreds of dollars. For the best information on credit card offers and interest rates, visit www.bankrate.com.

So many credit card companies are competing for your money that many are offering very low introductory rates. Again, you need to scrutinize them carefully—sometimes rates for balance transfers and cash advances are higher. And the introductory rate may jump by 10 percent or more after a few months. Obviously you want the card with the lowest introductory rate, and the longer the low rate lasts, the better. In any case, you don't want a card whose normal rate is above 10 percent.

Questions to Ask Potential Creditors Before Rolling Over a Balance to a Lower Rate

The following are questions you will need to ask prospective creditors before rolling over your balance, along with the acceptable answers.

How do you charge interest? On a single or double payment cycle?

One of the hidden costs of a credit card may be the way in which the company computes interest. The first method—and by far the better one for you—is to charge interest on the average daily balance, including new purchases. The second method, which is much less favorable, is the two-cycle average daily balance, including new purchases. Even if you never carry a balance from month to month, keep away from a company that calculates interest this way. You never know when you might need some emergency money for a few months, and this is an expensive way to get it. Always leave yourself the best option just in case.

What is the minimum percentage that the customer is required to pay every month?

The answer to this will vary from 1.5 percent of your balance to up to 4 percent. Here, for once, you want the figure to be higher, because the lower your required payment the longer it will take you to pay off the debt. In fact, it is essential that you *pay more than the minimum each month*. Still, the higher the minimum, the better.

If I carry a balance, is there a grace period on new purchases?

Most cards will charge you interest as soon as you make a purchase if you carry a balance, but there are some cards that do not, so keep your eyes peeled.

Is there an annual fee?

The only acceptable answer is no.

What is the cash advance fee, and what interest rate applies to cash advances?

This is where these companies can get you big-time. Even if your introductory rate is 5.9 percent, if you take out a cash advance, regardless of whether or not you owe a balance, many companies charge an additional fee of approximately 2.5 percent of the amount of each cash advance, up to a maximum fee of $20. Some cards will tell you to use the convenience checks that are supplied, but you have to ask about rates and fees, because many companies charge the same high rates even when you use their convenience checks.

Am I penalized if I don't carry a balance?

Most credit card companies make their money three ways: from the interest you pay on a balance; from annual fees, if applicable; and from the charges merchants pay for the privilege of letting customers use the card. You would think this would be enough. Some companies, however, are beginning to sneak in a little extra fee to those customers who don't carry a balance from one month to the next. Because more and more people are defaulting on consumer loans (credit cards, home equity, and car loans), companies are scrambling to think of new ways to charge you. Read all the tiny print every month, and watch for any undesirable changes in policy. When you spot one, switch cards.

Then there are these essential questions you must ask as well:

What is the current interest rate?
How long will this rate last?
By how much does the interest rate go up after the introductory period?

I'm asking you to pay very close attention to your credit cards. When can you stop being so vigilant? When your debt is gone and you've taken steps to see that it won't accumulate again.

Please use the worksheet on the next page when contacting potential creditors before rolling over a balance to get a lower rate.

ROLLING OVER BALANCE TO A LOWER
CREDIT CARD INTEREST RATE WORKSHEET

Company #1: _____

Company phone number: _____

Company address: _____

Contact: _____

What is the current interest rate? _____

How long will this rate last? _____

What does the interest rate go up to after the introductory period? _____

How do you charge interest: on a single or double payment cycle? _____

What is the minimum % that must be paid every month? _____

If I carry a balance, is there a grace period on new purchases? _____

Is there an annual fee? _____

What is the cash advance fee? _____

What interest rate applies to cash advances? _____

Am I penalized if I don't carry a balance? _____

Company #2: _____

Company phone number: _____

Company address: _____

Contact: _____

What is the current interest rate? _____

How long will this rate last? _____

What does the interest rate go up to after the introductory period? _____

How do you charge interest: on a single or double payment cycle? _____

What is the minimum % that must be paid every month? _____

If I carry a balance, is there a grace period on new purchases? _____

Is there an annual fee? _____

What is the cash advance fee? _____

What interest rate applies to cash advances? _____

Am I penalized if I don't carry a balance? _____

Company #3: _____

Company phone number: _____

Company address: _____

Contact: _____

What is the current interest rate? _____

How long will this rate last? _____

What does the interest rate go up to after the introductory period? _____

How do you charge interest: on a single or double payment cycle? _____

What is the minimum % that must be paid every month? _____

If I carry a balance, is there a grace period on new purchases? _____

Is there an annual fee? _____

What is the cash advance fee? _____

What interest rate applies to cash advances? _____

Am I penalized if I don't carry a balance? _____

✓

Action 4: Pay More Than the Minimum

If you have credit card debt, you need to pay more than the minimum amount due each month. Let me give you an example to show how large an impact this simple step can have on your debt load. Let's say you owe an average balance of $1,100 on a credit card that charges you 18.5 percent interest. If you pay the minimum each month, it will take you twelve years and six months to pay off the debt and will have cost you $2,480.94 in interest. If, however, you had just paid $10 more than the minimum amount due each month, you would have cut the payment period down to six years and cut the total interest payments to $1,805.57. That is a savings of $675.37.

TO PAY OFF A $1,100 DEBT AT 18.5%

Payment	Years to Pay Off	Interest
Minimum required	12½	$2,480.94
Minimum plus $10	6	$1,805.57

Action 5: Use Only Paper Money

By now you may be saying, "But I do not have extra cash every month to pay more than the minimum." You will have the extra cash if you begin to spend only paper money from now on. Let's say you go into a store and buy something for $4.50. You give the cashier a $5 bill and receive 50 cents in change. Put that change in your pocket. You go into another store and buy something for 50 cents. Rather than taking the change out of your pocket to pay for it, use a dollar bill and get another 50 cents in change. Each night, save your change in a cup or jar. If you do this, you will have an extra $40 to $60 a month to use toward your credit card payments and future savings. Take your change to the bank each month and get a cashier's check to pay toward your credit card balance.

Action 6: Call Your Creditors

If you know that you will not be able to make your monthly payment, immediately inform your credit card company or whatever entity you owe money to. Skipping payments or being late causes shame and disrespect in your life. And remember, disrespect repels money from you. Don't be embarrassed. With your new truth from Step 2 in hand, pick up the phone and call. You're in debt, that's all. You're not a failure or a bad person. If someone is rude to you, be very kind and gentle in return. Explain your situation. Perhaps you will have the money in two weeks. Or perhaps you can send $25. In any case, call your creditor before your creditor calls you.

If you're *not* late with your payments, call up your high-interest credit card companies anyway. Tell them you're considering switching to a better-value card, and see if they'll match a lower rate. You can negotiate with them, and often they will reduce your interest rate right on the spot. If they won't make good on your request, move the balance to a card that meets the criteria just discussed. If the high-interest companies won't give you as good a deal as you can get elsewhere, you're out of there.

Action 7: Switch to a Lower-Interest Card

Offers keep changing from company to company, so keep up-to-date on the best offers by checking a current issue of *SmartMoney* (www.smartmoney.com) or *Kiplinger's Personal Finance Magazine* (www.kiplinger.com). You can also check www.bankrate.com or my own Web site, www.suzeorman.com, in the resources section. If you have a blemish on your credit record, try to clean that up before you switch. Credit card companies don't like it if you've been even just one payment late, and for that reason alone a better company could turn you down.

A STEP-BY-STEP PLAN TO GET OUT OF CREDIT CARD DEBT

These are steps that many people have taken to get out of credit card debt. You can do it, too.

1. Figure out the absolute largest amount you can afford to pay monthly toward your credit card debt. Let's say that amount is $300. You may think this is a lot, but when you carry a lot of debt on at least several different cards, this is probably not much more than what all your minimum payments add up to.

> Write the largest amount you can put toward your debt in this box:

$

2. Review the list of creditors you made on page 92. On the worksheet below, list the creditors in descending order, with the highest interest rate first. Next, for each creditor list the <u>minimum payment plus $10</u>. If the minimum payment on one card is $50, write down $60, and so on. Find the total of all these and write it in the box marked *Total*.

EXAMPLE

Creditor	Minimum Payment + $10	Interest Rate	Balance Owed
Department store	75	21%	3,100
Visa	75	16.9%	6,300
Department store	50	7.9%	2,200
MasterCard	50	5.9%	1,800
TOTAL	$250		$13,400

YOUR DEBT

Creditor	Minimum Payment + $10	Interest Rate	Balance Owed
Card #1			
Card #2			
Card #3			
Card #4			
TOTAL	$		

3. Take the largest amount you can put toward your debt, the number that you wrote down in the first step of this plan to get out of debt, and subtract the minimum-plus-$10 payment total, the number that you wrote down in the second step. Let's say that you decided you can put $300 a month toward eradicating your debt and that the minimum-plus-$10 for all of your credit cards came to a total of $250. This leaves you with an extra $50 to pay on your credit cards.

EXAMPLE		YOUR DEBT	
Largest Amount toward Debt	$300	Largest Amount toward Debt	
minus (–)		minus (–)	
Minimum Payment Total	$250	Minimum Payment Total	
Extra to Pay Debt	$50	Extra to Pay Debt	

4. Now take the "extra to pay debt" and each month put it toward the card with the highest interest rate. Repeat until the first card is paid off. When the card is paid off, call the company and close the account.

5. Now start over again with the creditor charging the next highest interest rate. Stick with the same total of largest amount you can pay toward your debt (unless you can raise it!). For each of your remaining cards, take the minimum payment plus $10 and write it in the minimum payment box. Then find the total and write it in the box marked *Total*. Let's say that figure is now $200 a month. Subtract this from the $300 you have allocated a month, and you are left with $100. Add the $100 to the amount you are paying on the card that is now charging you the highest interest rate. When the card is paid off, call the company and close the account. Then start all over again with the third card.

YOUR REMAINING DEBT

Creditor	Minimum Payment + $10	Interest Rate	Balance Owed
Card #2			
Card #3			
Card #4			
TOTAL	$		

This whole process may take months or it may take years, but with each payment you will be closer to becoming debt-free—at which time you'll be free to pay *yourself* more and more. Look at the statements carefully each time; keep transferring accounts for the best interest rate deals as necessary, and take pleasure and pride each time the amount due is smaller. With each payment you are that much closer to Financial Freedom.

BORROWING TO PAY OFF CREDIT CARD DEBT

Another way to get out of credit card debt is to borrow money from your 401(k) plan if you have one, or take out a home equity loan or home equity line of credit. Before you use those sources of money to pay off your credit card debt, I would like you to answer the following questions.

	YES	NO
Do you consistently go over the credit limit on your credit cards?	___	___
Are you late in your payments?	___	___
Do you owe a person money you have not paid back?	___	___
Do you feel that your spending is still out of control?	___	___

If you answered yes to the majority of these questions, it is not wise to borrow from your 401(k) or your home equity to pay off your credit card debt. The reason is as follows.

Just because you have paid off your credit card debt does not mean that you have dealt with the emotional and financial issues that got you into credit card debt to begin with. If you take a home equity line of credit to pay off your credit card debt, you have transferred that debt onto your home. You will then have a sizable sum of money available via the credit maximums on your credit cards because you just paid off all of your credit cards. In most cases, unless you have dealt with your debt issues, you will charge up your credit cards to the maximum again. Only this time you will also owe on your home equity loan. You are now in double trouble! If, however, you understand why you got into credit card debt to begin with, you can be respectful of your current financial situation. If you have been able to keep your financial commitment to yourself and create your new truth(s) and if you have done the exercises and been honest with yourself, then it might make sense for you to look into refinancing your credit card debt using a home equity line of credit. Very seldom, however, does it make sense to borrow money from a 401(k) plan to pay off credit card debt.

Borrowing from Your 401(k) to Pay Off Credit Card Debt

You may be eligible to borrow from yourself to pay off your credit cards through your 401(k) plan at work. Many employers will let you borrow up to 50 percent of the money you have in your plan, up to $50,000, to buy a house or pay off bills or for other situations that qualify. Please be careful about doing this. The supposed upside is that when you borrow money from a 401(k), you have five years to pay back the money (rather than the forty years it could take you by paying the minimum on some credit cards) so, presumably, you'll be disciplined into getting out of debt more quickly. In addition, the interest you pay goes right back to yourself. That's right, it's your money, you've borrowed it from yourself, and you're paying it back directly into your account; all the payments plus interest go to you. Usually you will pay yourself about 2 percent above the prime rate, which is the basic interest rate set by the banks for their best customers.

But the downside is this: When you borrow money from your 401(k), you are losing out on the growth potential of the money you plan to retire on. So it's a decision to be made cautiously and wisely.

Another very serious consideration is that if you take out a loan on your 401(k), you will be taxed twice on the amount you borrow. Yes, that's right. You will be paying back money that you never paid taxes on with money you have paid taxes on, and then, when you take the money out at retirement, you will pay taxes on it again. That really makes no sense. So you have to think carefully before you take out a loan from a 401(k). Not only are you losing growth on this money, but you are subjecting your money to double taxation.

Another potential downside is that if you happen to leave the job or get fired, the money you borrowed is due in one lump sum at that time. If you can't pay it back, you'll pay taxes on the money as if it were ordinary income; if you're under the age of fifty-nine and a half, you may also have to pay a 10 percent penalty on the amount you haven't paid back. If you are thinking of taking out a loan, and there is a possibility you may leave your current employer, you should reconsider. Before you take out the loan, make sure you understand what you would have to do if you were to leave your job.

Home Equity Loans to Pay Off Credit Cards

Another alternative, if you're really in credit card trouble, is to take out a home equity loan to pay off your debt. A home equity loan can have its advantages. The loan may be at a lower interest rate than your credit card debt, and often home-loan interest payments are tax-deductible, so you'll have converted a high-interest, non-tax-deductible debt to one that has lower interest and is tax-deductible.

The amount of money that you can take out of your home with this kind of loan is based on a percentage of the equity that you have in your home. Equity is the difference between what your house is worth and how much you owe on your mortgage. In other words, if your house is worth $200,000 and you have a mortgage of $150,000, it means that you have about $50,000 equity in your home.

Can you then take out a $50,000 home equity loan? No, most banks will let you borrow a total of only 80 percent of the value of your house, minus all current mortgages. If your house is worth $200,000, 80 percent of its value is $160,000. Subtract the $150,000 you owe on the first mortgage, and this gives you the amount you can get on a home equity loan if you qualify: in this case, $10,000.

Please note, however, that when you convert credit card debt into a home equity loan you are converting an unsecured loan on your credit card into a loan secured with your house. If you cannot pay your credit card debt, you will lose your credit card privileges. If you cannot pay a home loan, you may lose your house. This is a huge difference. Please be careful.

Equity Line of Credit

Another option is an equity line of credit, which enables you to borrow money as you need it against your house. The interest on an equity line of credit usually varies according to what general interest rates are doing. Also, the payback period is not set—so be sure you're very disciplined if you are considering this alternative. With this type of loan you do not have to pay back principal each month if you don't want to. You can pay just the interest, if that better meets your needs. (A home equity loan, on the other hand, works pretty much like a regular mortgage. You can get a fixed interest rate and pay back the loan over a fixed period of time, usually from five to fifteen years.)

If, on the other hand, you are eligible to *refinance* your original mortgage at a lower interest rate, your best bet may be to refinance. It will depend on the amount of money you want to take out of your home and the interest rate environment. Please check this out.

IF YOU ARE IN SEVERE DEBT

Cut Up Your Cards

All credit cards must be cut up NOW! If you are not willing to do this, it's a sign that you need some serious help. It means you still don't understand the implications of having debt of this kind—and that you are still being disrespectful to yourself and to your money. People are often afraid not to carry credit cards, and if you feel this way, by all means carry one for emergencies, but reduce the credit available to you by calling the company and asking to have the limit lowered—it takes just one simple phone call. Pick the amount of credit you would like to have in case of an emergency ($500 or $1,000), and ask the company to set the limit there. Or carry an American Express card, the basic version that must be paid off in full every month. You wouldn't stock the kitchen with cookies if you were dieting, would you? Why keep credit around that you don't need and don't want to use, if the temptation might get you into trouble?

If You Need Help

If you need help managing your debt, you might want to check out a nonprofit organization that has been set up to help educate you on your money and, at the same time, help you with a payment plan so that all of your cards will be paid off within five years, at most.

My favorite group is known as NFCC, or National Foundation for Credit Counseling (also known as CCCS, or Consumer Credit Counseling Service). To find an office near you, call (800) 388-2777. Or visit the Web site: www.nfcc.org. If you need serious help managing your debt, you should check out a program such as this.

Here is how such programs work: You hand over all your credit cards to them, and for a fee of about ten dollars a month you will give them one check and they will pay your creditors for you. Most likely they will be able to get you a lower interest rate than you are currently paying. They can do this because they have deals with many of the credit card companies themselves, so they are able to negotiate a better interest rate with your current cards than you may be able to. In fact, it is the credit card companies that help to fund most of these organizations, for the card companies believe that it is better to get some of their money back than none at all. For most people with out-of-control debt, these organizations are a great help—but they do have drawbacks. In most cases, for seven years your credit report will have a line stating that you paid through NFCC. This may help or hurt you in getting additional credit; some companies look at it as a negative and some think of it as a positive because you're taking control of your debt. In any case, you should speak to a credit counselor about your specific debt situation.

CREDIT BUREAUS AND CREDIT REPORTS

I recommend that you check your credit report periodically in order to make sure that all the information, including closed accounts, etc., is accurate. At your request, a credit bureau must give you the information in your file—and a list of everyone who has requested it recently. If you have been turned down for credit because of information supplied by the credit bureau, there is no charge for the report if you request it within sixty days of receiving notice of the action. You can apply for this through the credit card company or the bank that turned you down. Or for a nominal fee, generally around $8, you can request a copy through one of the credit bureaus listed on the next page.

If you find a mistake on your credit report, fill out the "Request for Reinvestigation" form that accompanies the credit report. If you do not receive this form, write to the credit bureau and ask for one. On the form, list each incorrect item and explain exactly what is wrong. Be sure to make a copy of the form before sending it back. The reinvestigation is free. The following Web sites are also helpful in correcting a credit report: www.mycreditfile.com and www.righttoknow.com.

Below are the addresses, phone numbers, and Web sites of the three major credit bureaus.

Equifax (formerly CBI/Equifax)
P.O. Box 740241
Atlanta, GA 30374-0341
(800) 685-1111
(800) 997-2493 for residents of Colorado, Georgia, Maryland,
Massachusetts, New Jersey, or Vermont
www.equifax.com/consumer/consumer.html

Experian (formerly TRW Information Systems, Inc.)
P.O. Box 2104
Allen, TX 75013-2104
(888) 397-3742
www.experian.com

Trans Union Corporation
Consumer Disclosure Center
P.O. Box 403
Springfield, PA 19064-0390
(800) 888-4213 to get your credit report
(800) 916-8800 to ask questions about your credit report
www.tuc.com

Credit Scoring

Credit scoring is a numerical computation a potential lender uses in an effort to predict how risky it might be to lend you money, whether in the form of credit or a loan. When the application arrives at a bank or a credit card company, an employee enters all the pertinent information from your application into the company computer. The company's computer dials up the credit bureau's computer, which assembles your credit report on the spot. The lender's computer analyzes the combined data from your application form and your credit report and comes up with a numerical score, commonly called a FICO score, that guides the lender in deciding whether or not to approve a loan or extend you credit.

FICO scores take into account information about checking and savings account balances and activity, outstanding debt, and payment records. The better your history, the higher your FICO score. Scores range from 300 to 850. To be approved for a loan or a line of credit, you want a FICO score of 650 or higher. If your score is below that, you are considered at risk for default, and most companies will not take a chance on you. If you score between 620 and 650, you will stay in a kind of limbo until you have provided the lender with further documentation. If you want to check your FICO score, you can now do so on the Web at www.myfico.com or www.equifax.com; the cost is $12.95, and a copy of your credit report is included.

Adding Yourself to Your Payroll

It is not respectful of yourself, of others, or of your money not to plan for your future. It is not respectful of yourself, of others, or of your money not to take full advantage of the 401(k)s, IRAs, and other retirement plans that are available to you. It is not respectful of yourself, of others, and of your money not to face your debt, not to learn the basics of investing, and not to guard your money, making sure that every penny you're spending is a penny that must be spent. What day you pay your bills, when you send in your taxes, and what hidden costs you pay for your checking account all can make a difference in how much money you keep in your pocket and how much money gets attracted to you. We all think that a bigger paycheck would be the answer to our financial woes, but that is rarely the case. Respect starts with the money you are earning right now and what you do with it.

> **THE THIRD LAW OF FINANCIAL FREEDOM, PART 1:**
> The More You Make, the More You Spend

Making Your Mind Your Friend

Your mind is the most powerful tool you have. You must make it believe that you earn less than you do so that you will naturally spend less.

> **THE THIRD LAW OF FINANCIAL FREEDOM, PART 2:**
> The Less You Think You Make,
> the Less You Will Spend

Your mind believes that if you bring home a monthly paycheck of $3,000, then you have $3,000 to spend. And you'll spend it, all of it. If you get a raise and start bringing home $4,000 a month, you'll spend all of that, too, and wonder how on earth you managed on less; but if you start bringing home $3,500 a month instead, your mind will adjust to that amount. The lesson: Put your money safely away before you ever see it.

You won't be depriving yourself. You'll be paying yourself. You'll be on your own payroll and you will soon be able to enjoy two of life's great pleasures: counting your money as it grows and dreaming of how you'll spend it when the time comes.

TIME AND YOUR 401(K) EXERCISE

Whether we want to accept it or not, all of us one day are going to have to live on the money we have earned rather than on the money we are earning. The time to start planning for that day is now. Please answer yes or no to the following questions.

	YES	NO
Are you currently participating (or planning to participate when you are eligible) in a 401(k), 403(b), or SIMPLE retirement plan at your place of employment?	___	___
Are you contributing the maximum that you are allowed by law to your retirement plan?	___	___

If you did not answer yes to both of these questions, let me tell you right now that, unless you are in credit card debt, in my opinion, you are making one of the biggest financial mistakes possible.

Let me ask you one more question: If you cannot afford to put money away for your retirement because you do not have enough money to pay your bills while you have a paycheck coming in, how are you going to pay those exact same bills when you no longer have a paycheck coming in? Put your answer in the box below.

How will I pay my bills when I'm retired?

```



```
✓

The only answer that is appropriate is that you will not be able to. You may say, "But Suze, I can barely afford to pay my bills as it is. How do you expect me to live today and still put money away for my retirement?" Even on a modest salary, if you start now you can put aside an impressive amount of money. So once again, I urge you to start saving today for your tomorrows.

If You Are Not in Credit Card Debt

If you are not in credit card debt and are signed up at work for a 401(k), 403(b), or SIMPLE plan, I want you to go to your human resources office and up your contribution to the maximum possible. If you have not signed up for your retirement plan, please do so now. If you are self-employed or your place of employment doesn't offer a 401(k) or similar plan, please read on and take the actions that are right for you.

Contributing to Your Retirement Plan if You Have Credit Card Debt

If you have credit card debt and if you are eligible to invest in your 401(k), I would like to ask you the following questions. Please answer yes or no.

	YES	NO
Is the interest rate on your credit card debt higher than the average rate of return on your 401(k) plan?	____	____
Do you hate having credit card debt?	____	____
		✓

If you answered yes to both of the questions above I want you to begin changing the way you contribute to your 401(k) based on whether or not your company matches your 401(k) contribution.

Company <u>Does Not Match</u> Your 401(k) Contribution and Interest Rate on Your Credit Card Is Higher Than the Return on Your 401(k) Plan	Company <u>Does Match</u> Your 401(k) Contribution and Interest Rate on Your Credit Card Is Higher Than the Return on Your 401(k) Plan	Company <u>Does Match</u> Your 401(k) Contribution and Interest Rate on Your Credit Card Is Lower Than the Return on Your 401(k) Plan
You should stop contributing to your 401(k) plan and take all of that money that you would have been contributing to your 401(k) and put that toward paying off your credit card debt. After your debt is paid in full you can then go back to contributing to your 401(k).	You should still contribute to your 401(k) plan up to the point of the match. After you have reached the maximum amount of money that your company will match, then and only then should you stop contributing to your 401(k) and take that money and put it toward paying off the debt.	If you do not mind having credit card debt and you are forty years of age or younger, then you should continue to invest fully in your 401(k) plan, at least to the level of the match, and pay off your credit card debt at the same time.

Commitment to Contribute to Retirement Plan

Please make a commitment to yourself to contribute the most respectful amount to your retirement plan and to take the steps to do so this week.

> I promise, if I am not in credit card debt, that this week I will increase my contribution to the maximum in my retirement plan.
>
> If I am in credit card debt, and if my company matches my retirement plan contribution, I will contribute up to the match. I will then evaluate how I feel about my credit card debt, compare the interest rate on my credit card to the return on my 401(k) or similar retirement plan, and respectfully put additional money toward paying off my credit card debt and/or toward my 401(k) or similar retirement plan.
>
> _____   _____   _____
> Date I promise to   Signature   Today's date
> take action

✓

THE FOURTH LAW OF FINANCIAL FREEDOM:
It's Not What You Make,
It's What You Get to Keep

Employer-Sponsored Retirement Plan Basics: How They Work

The plans known as 401(k), 403(b), and SIMPLE allow you to contribute a percentage of your salary, usually around 15 percent, into a tax-advantaged retirement savings plan. A 401(k), which takes its exciting name from a section of the tax code, is an all-around plan that almost any company can enter into. A 403(b) plan is what you have if you work for a nonprofit organization, such as a hospital, university, or research organization. The 401(k) and 403(b) plans work in the same way. A SIMPLE works differently. The acronym stands for Savings Incentive Match Plan for Employees. The plan can be adopted by firms that employ one hundred or fewer employees with at least $5,000 in compensation for the previous year and that do not maintain another employer-sponsored retirement plan. On the following page is a quick reference guide to employer-sponsored retirement plans.

QUICK REFERENCE GUIDE: EMPLOYER-SPONSORED RETIREMENT PLANS

	401(k)	403(b)	SIMPLE
Definition	A voluntary retirement plan offered to employees of companies that allows up to a certain percentage of employees' pretax pay to be set aside and invested within the retirement plan.	A voluntary retirement plan offered to employees of public institutions such as hospitals and schools that allows up to a certain percentage of employees' pretax pay to be set aside and invested within the retirement plan.	A voluntary retirement plan (Savings Incentive Match Plan for Employees) set up by a small business firm for its employees. Employees receive some level of matching contribution from employer.
What is the maximum contribution?	Year / Under Age 50 / Over Age 50 2002 $11,000 $12,000 2003 12,000 14,000 2004 13,000 16,000 2005 14,000 18,000 2006 15,000 20,000 After 2006, increases will be indexed in $500 increments based upon inflation.	Year / Under Age 50 / Over Age 50 2002 $11,000 $12,000 2003 12,000 14,000 2004 13,000 16,000 2005 14,000 18,000 2006 15,000 20,000 After 2006, increases will be indexed in $500 increments based upon inflation.	Year / Under Age 50 / Over Age 50 2002 $ 7,000 $ 7,500 2003 8,000 9,000 2004 9,000 10,500 2005 10,000 12,000 2006 12,500 After 2005 for those under 50 and after 2006 for those over 50, increases will be indexed in $500 increments based upon inflation.
When and how am I taxed?	Taxes are deferred until you take your money out, at which time it will be taxed as ordinary income.	Taxes are deferred until you take your money out, at which time it will be taxed as ordinary income.	Taxes are deferred until you take your money out, at which time it will be taxed as ordinary income.
When can I withdraw funds?	In most cases you cannot withdraw the funds prior to age 59½ without paying a 10% federal penalty, as well as a state income tax penalty on the amount withdrawn.	In most cases you cannot withdraw the funds prior to age 59½ without paying a 10% federal penalty, as well as a state income tax penalty on the amount withdrawn.	In most cases you cannot withdraw the funds prior to age 59½ without paying a 10% federal penalty, as well as a state income tax penalty on the amount withdrawn. In addition, if you take out funds within the first two years you participate in the plan, an early withdrawal tax of 25% will apply.

Individual Retirement Accounts

In addition to an employer's retirement plan, you can also have a traditional IRA, or individual retirement account. However, if you are covered by an employer's plan, whether or not you can deduct your contributions depends on your income level. (If you are not covered by an employer's plan, you can deduct your contributions no matter what your income, and you can always open and contribute to a traditional non-deductible IRA.) There are income limits for deducting your contributions to a traditional IRA if you are part of an employer's retirement plan. For single people covered by an employer's retirement plan, the deductibility phases out between a modified adjusted gross income (MAGI) of $34,000 and $44,000 in 2002, $40,000 and $50,000 in 2003, $45,000 and $55,000 in 2004, and $50,000 and $60,000 in 2005 and later. If you are married and file jointly and are both covered by an employer's plan, the deductibility phases out between a MAGI of $54,000 and $64,000 in 2002, $60,000 and $70,000 in 2003, $65,000 and $75,000 in 2004, $70,000 and $80,000 in 2005, $75,000 and $85,000 in 2006, and $80,000 and $100,000 in 2007 and later. If you are married and not covered by an employer's plan, but your spouse is covered by an employer's plan, the deductibility phases out between a MAGI of $150,000 and $160,000. Under any circumstances, the maximum amount you can contribute for 2002–2004 is $3,000 if you are under age fifty, or $3,500 if you are fifty or older.

Besides a traditional IRA, you can also contribute to a Roth IRA if you meet the Roth income qualifications. For 2002–2004, single taxpayers whose MAGI is less than $95,000 per year, and married couples filing a joint return who have a combined annual MAGI of less than $150,000, can contribute up to $3,000 each if they are under fifty, or $3,500 if they are over fifty. Your eligibility to contribute the full $3,000 (or $3,500 if you are over fifty) is phased out between an income of $95,000 and $110,000 for single taxpayers and between $150,000 and $160,000 for married taxpayers filing jointly. After those income amounts, you are not eligible for a Roth IRA.

With a Roth IRA, contributions are not tax-deductible, but your contributions can grow tax-free rather than tax-deferred. That means that when you withdraw money from a Roth IRA at retirement, you will not owe any taxes on that money, no matter how greatly the money has grown in value, provided you have followed IRS guidelines. In addition, with a Roth IRA, you do not have to wait until you are fifty-nine and a half to begin taking withdrawals, as you do with a traditional IRA; you can take out your original contribution anytime you want, regardless of your age, without taxes or penalties. Any gains your contributions earn, however, must stay in the Roth IRA until you have turned fifty-nine and a half, and have held your account for more than five years, in order for you to withdraw them without taxes or penalties. Earnings from a Roth IRA can be withdrawn penalty-free if you become disabled or die.

Please note: You can have both a traditional IRA and a Roth IRA, but you can contribute only the maximum amount allowed each year to all your IRAs put together, no matter how many you have or what kind they are. For 2002, that amount is $3,000 if you are under fifty and $3,500 if you are fifty or older.

Here is a comparison of traditional IRAs and Roth IRAs:

IRA COMPARISONS

	Traditional IRA	Spousal IRA	Roth IRA
Tax-deductible contributions	Yes (in most cases)	Yes (in most cases)	No
Taxable at withdrawal	Yes	Yes	No (if you meet qualifications)
10% penalty for premature withdrawal	Yes, prior to age $59\frac{1}{2}$	Yes, prior to age $59\frac{1}{2}$	Yes, for earnings withdrawn prior to age $59\frac{1}{2}$ and before five years have passed from when the Roth was funded. Original contributions can be withdrawn penalty-free and tax-free at any time.
Mandatory withdrawal age	$70\frac{1}{2}$	$70\frac{1}{2}$	No
Penalty-free withdrawals	$10,000 for first-time home buyers, or unlimited for educational purposes	$10,000 for first-time home buyers, or unlimited for educational purposes	$10,000 for first-time home buyers, or unlimited for educational purposes. Original contribution can be withdrawn tax-free at any time and for any purpose.
Maximum contribution	Year / Under Age 50 / Over Age 50 2002–04 $3,000 $3,500 2005 4,000 4,500 2006 4,000 5,000 2007 4,000 5,000 2008 5,000 6,000 After 2008, increases will be indexed in $500 increments based upon inflation.	Year / Under Age 50 / Over Age 50 2002–04 $3,000 $3,500 2005 4,000 4,500 2006 4,000 5,000 2007 4,000 5,000 2008 5,000 6,000 After 2008, increases will be indexed in $500 increments based upon inflation.	Year / Under Age 50 / Over Age 50 2002–04 $3,000 $3,500 2005 4,000 4,500 2006 4,000 5,000 2007 4,000 5,000 2008 5,000 6,000 After 2008, increases will be indexed in $500 increments based upon inflation.

IRA Conversions and Qualifications

If your yearly adjusted gross income is $100,000 or less, the government also allows you to convert any or all of your traditional IRAs into a Roth IRA. If you do this, what you need to know is that even though you may be under the age of fifty-nine and a half when you take the money out of your traditional IRA to convert to a Roth, the 10 percent penalty tax will not apply—but you *will* owe ordinary income tax on any money that you converted.

Roth Conversions

When you convert money from a traditional IRA to a Roth IRA, the withdrawal privileges should be noted. The money that you originally converted—that is, both earnings and contributions—has got to stay in the Roth account for five years or until you are fifty-nine and a half, whichever comes first, before you can withdraw it without taxes or penalties. You do not, however, have to be fifty-nine and a half to withdraw the converted amount to avoid the 10 percent penalty, you just have to have met the five-year holding requirement. So let's say that you are thirty-nine and you convert $50,000 from a traditional IRA to a Roth. That $50,000 has to stay in the Roth IRA for at least five years. After that time, even though you will just be forty-four, you can withdraw all $50,000 without any taxes or penalties. The earnings on that $50,000, however, cannot be withdrawn without penalties or taxes until you have reached age fifty-nine and a half.

401(k) Plans Versus Roth IRAs

Are you eligible for a company retirement plan like a 401(k) and do you also qualify to fund a Roth IRA? If so, deciding which one to fund first can be confusing. It's best to fund both to the maximum, if you can. But if money is tight and it is an either/or situation, then this is what you should do: If you have a 401(k) or 403(b) plan where your employer matches your contribution (meaning that for every dollar you put into your retirement plan at work, the employer puts money in for you as well), fund your 401(k) or 403(b) up to the point of the match. Once you reach the point where the employer is no longer matching your contribution (or if your 401(k) or 403(b) plan does not have a matching program to begin with), figure out what tax bracket you are in. If you are making a lot of money and in a high tax bracket and you like the investment choices that your retirement plan at work offers, continue to fund your 401(k)/403(b) plan to the max. Then fund your Roth IRA if you can. If, however, you are not currently in a very high tax bracket or you do not like the investment choices within your retirement plan at work, first fund your Roth IRA, and then, if you have the money, fund the 401(k)/403(b) plan at work.

If you have been investing in a non-tax-deductible IRA, you should definitely consider switching to a Roth IRA, if you're eligible; for most people, the Roth makes the non-tax-deductible IRA obsolete. If you are not covered by a company plan and can really use the tax write-off from a traditional IRA deposit right now, but you are a spender and not a saver and will fritter away the tax savings from a traditional IRA instead of investing them each year, then you might want to lean more toward the Roth IRA as a savings against future taxes. In other words, pass up the current tax savings for the future big picture.

If you are very young, just starting out in your career, and in a low tax bracket, by all means look into a Roth IRA, which can jump-start your retirement savings by a lot, even if you switch tactics later. Let's say that from ages twenty-one to thirty you invested $3,000 in a Roth IRA averaging an annual return of 10 percent every year, and then you never deposited another cent into that account and just let it grow. At age fifty-nine and a half, you'd have $711,000 that you could access totally tax-free. If you consider that all a traditional, deductible IRA would have saved you in taxes (if you are in a 15 percent tax bracket) would be around $450 a year, or $4,500 over ten years, you can see that you'd be better off in a Roth. It makes no sense to have to pay taxes on $711,000 later on in life (when you might be in a very high tax bracket) just to have saved $4,500 over ten years early in your career. By the way, if your tax bracket changes and you want the deduction of a regular IRA, you can make that change anytime you want. Rather than making a deposit into your Roth IRA that year, open a traditional IRA.

Maximizing the Impact of a Roth or a Traditional IRA

Most people wait until just before they file their taxes in April to contribute to their IRA. This is a mistake and an incredible waste of an opportunity to let your money grow. For the tax year 2002, if you qualify, you have the right to put up to $3,000 in your IRA in January 2002. If you possibly can, you should put that money away at the beginning of the year rather than at the tax deadline.

If you invest your $3,000 in January 2002 and that money sits there, averaging an 8 percent return, by the time April 15, 2003, comes along you will have $230 more in the account. If you simply keep this up, you'll have thousands of dollars more over the years you maintain this account.

Look at the larger picture. If you put $3,000 away each year for the next twenty-five years and this money averages an 8 percent return, after twenty-five years you will have $235,647 in your IRA. If instead you waited to make this contribution until the end of every December, you'd have $219,317, which is $16,330 less.

If you don't have $3,000 at the beginning of the year, and so can't make the investment all at once, start putting $250 (or whatever you can) each month into your IRA. Continue to do so for the next twenty-five years and you will still come out better than if you had waited to do it in one lump sum at each year's end. How much better? About $7,100 better. You will have $226,451 rather than $219,317.

Retirement Plans for the Self-Employed

If you are self-employed, you also have excellent options for funding your retirement. You can open up an SEP-IRA or a Keogh. Either one is a great way to save for retirement. In order for you to qualify for these retirement accounts, your earnings must be reported on Form 1099-MISC or be earned as fees for services you've provided. In both plans, as of 2002 the limit on your annual contributions will be up to 25 percent of your net earnings, up to a maximum of $40,000. If you have people working for you, after a certain period of time you'll have to fund the SEP-IRA or Keogh plan for them as well. If you are thinking of setting up an SEP-IRA or a Keogh, it's best to consult an accountant familiar with these plans.

TIME CREATES MONEY

Employed, self-employed—it doesn't matter; the key is to start to save as soon as you can. When it comes to money, time is probably the most important factor in the growth process. The more you save and the more time you give to your money to grow, the more you will attract and create large sums. The amount you have accumulated when retirement comes will determine what kind of lifestyle you will then be able to afford.

TIME QUIZ

1. If at age twenty-five you start putting $100 a month into an account that averages a 12 percent return, how much will you have at sixty-five? _____

2. If you start ten years later, at age thirty-five, how much will you have at sixty-five?

_____

3. If you start twenty years later, at age forty-five, how much will you have at sixty-five?

_____

Answers: 1. $1 Million   2. $300,000   3. $97,000

Time accounts for the difference. For every year you wait to take the step of establishing respect for your life and your future, it costs you thousands of dollars. In this scenario, by waiting twenty years—from age twenty-five to age forty-five—you will have lost almost $900,000. Why does a difference of just a few years make such a big difference in the financial big picture?   ✓

Compound Interest

The answer is one of the secrets of financial success: Compound interest multiplies your money. When you leave your money invested over time, the amounts of money that your contributions are generating on their own are the worker bees in your money hive. For instance, let's say you are investing $6,000 a year, and that $6,000 is earning 8 percent. Let's assume that your investment will be able to average that 8 percent over the next twenty years, and that you continue to add $6,000 at the beginning of every year. There will come a point in time when the earnings on your account will add up, by themselves, to generate more every year than the $6,000 you are contributing. This is when those worker bees really start to make that money honey.

Take a look at the table on the next page and see how many years it will take before you earn as much in interest every year as you are putting in. Look a little further down the road, and you'll see that in just a few more years you could be earning three times more a year in interest than what you are contributing.

Why? Because of the magic of compounding! It is for this reason and this reason alone that you cannot afford to let one year pass without making a contribution to your retirement plan. The wonderful effects of compounding are too compelling to ignore.

EXAMPLE OF HOW COMPOUND INTEREST WORKS

Year	401(k) Yearly Contribution	Interest Earned at 8% per Annum	
1	$6,000	$ 480	
2	6,000	998	
3	6,000	1,558	
4	6,000	2,163	
5	6,000	2,816	
6	6,000	3,521	
7	6,000	4,283	
8	6,000	5,106	
9	6,000	5,994	Interest now equals your contribution
10	6,000	6,954	
11	6,000	7,990	
12	6,000	9,109	
13	6,000	10,318	
14	6,000	11,623	
15	6,000	13,033	Interest is more than twice your contribution
16	6,000	14,556	
17	6,000	16,200	
18	6,000	17,976	Interest is three times your contribution
19	6,000	19,894	
20	6,000	21,966	

Since time is of the essence, you have got to start NOW to multiply your money.

PUTTING YOUR MONEY TO WORK FOR YOU OUTSIDE OF RETIREMENT PLANS

Would you throw a dollar on the street for someone else to pick up? I doubt it. Yet without even knowing it, you may be throwing away hundreds or thousands of dollars in found money just by the way you are dealing with your bank accounts and other savings vehicles. Most people try to set up their savings for convenience, to make things easy. But easy can be costly. Respecting yourself and your money means wanting to put every penny you can to work for you. Respect attracts money, remember? Without knowing it, you might have "found money" right now, a few hundred dollars here, a few hundred there, or more. Wouldn't you like to find it? You can if you are just willing to look. If you are willing to rearrange the pieces of your financial life just a little, you'll be able to see the solution to the puzzle—and find the money. A money market account is a great way to start.

Your money needs to be in a holding place where it will earn the most it can for you—it's that simple. So wherever your money is now, ask yourself the following questions:

	Checking	Savings
How much is the money in my checking and savings account earning?		

	Checking	Other Sources
How much does the bank charge me monthly for checks or other service fees?		

If you don't know the answer, call up your bank and find out right now and write the amount in the boxes above.

Now I want you to do some comparison shopping and see if you get a higher interest rate somewhere else, whether you can pay less in fees, and whether you can establish an account that is just as safe and convenient. One of the comparisons should be at another bank, and the other should be at a discount brokerage firm like Charles Schwab, Fidelity, or Muriel Siebert.

✓

ARE YOU MAKING THE MOST OF YOUR MONEY?

	Current Account	Comparison #1	Comparison #2
Company			
Interest rate on checking account			
Interest rate on savings account			
Interest rate on money market account			
Fee for checks			
Service fees			

Now please answer the following question:

	YES	NO
Do you have a money market account?	_____	_____

If the answer is no, I would like you to seriously considering opening one. The difference in interest rates between a traditional savings account and a money market account can be significant over time.

✓

Money Market Accounts

A money market account can be opened through a bank, a full-service brokerage firm, a discount brokerage firm, a mutual fund company, or a credit union. It works like a bank account. You keep your money there, and you can write checks against it. There are various restrictions, but you can usually find a money market account to suit you.

Questions for Money Market Account Providers

The following are questions you must ask potential money market providers and the acceptable answers that you should receive.

What is the minimum deposit I need to open up the account?

The answer should be that you can open a great account for between a $1,000 and a $5,000 minimum.

What is the minimum balance, if any, required to keep it open?

The answer you want to hear is none.

Am I required to purchase securities in order to maintain the account? If I don't plan to do so, will you charge me a fee eventually?

Some money market accounts require you to make a transaction—buy a stock, buy into a mutual fund—in order to maintain the account, or at least to maintain it free if you don't keep a balance above the minimum amount needed. Others don't. This is not a big deal and may encourage you to test the investment waters, but if it makes you uncomfortable, the answer you want to hear is no.

Are there expenses associated with the account that I may have to pay?

The answer may be yes. Be careful of this, especially in a low-interest-rate environment, because "expense ratios" may be higher than your interest rate, leaving you with little or no profit.

Do you issue a debit and an ATM card?

The answer should be yes, or else that you can use your debit card like an ATM card.

Are there fees if I use my ATM card? What are they?

If there are fees, they should not be more than a few dollars per transaction.

Is there a maximum number of checks I can write every month?

The answer should be no.

Is there a minimum amount for which checks can be written?

The answer should be no.

Do you return my canceled checks or simply send me an itemized statement every month?

Either way is okay, but most will simply send you an itemized statement.

At the end of the year, do you give me a summary of every check I've written?

The answer you want is yes.

What interest rate are you currently paying, or what is your seven-day yield or the amount in interest you have paid for the past week?

The higher the figure the better.

How do you credit this interest?

You want to hear that the interest is credited daily.

MONEY MARKET ACCOUNT WORKSHEET

What is the minimum deposit I need to open up the account?	
What is the minimum balance, if any, required to keep it open?	
Am I required to purchase securities in order to maintain the account?	
If I don't plan to purchase securities, will you charge me a fee eventually?	
Do you issue a debit and an ATM card?	
Are there fees if I use my ATM card? What are they?	
Is there a maximum number of checks I can write every month?	
Is there a minimum amount for which checks can be written?	
What is the expense ratio, if any?	
Do you return my canceled checks or simply send me an itemized statement every month?	
At the end of the year, do you give me a summary of every check I've written?	
What interest rate are you currently paying, or what is your seven-day yield or the amount in interest you have paid for the past week?	
How do you credit this interest?	

✓

The Best Place to Open a Money Market Account

Some of the best-rated money market accounts can be found with Vanguard (Prime Money Market Fund) and Charles Schwab (Value Advantage). To get the best up-to-date information on money market rates, visit www.bankrate.com. If you write more than fifteen checks each month, you may find that it is just as cost effective to keep your checking account where it is and to move only your savings to a money market account. There may be other rules governing the account—minimum balance, minimum you can write checks for—so keep your needs in mind when setting up the account.

REVIEW

With this step the path to Financial Freedom is coming into view. You're on course, you're almost there. Now you can clear up the debt that has preoccupied you and weighed you down in fear. The future looks clearer, too, doesn't it? You can see that, once you've taken the actions you need to take, you will be able to create enough for tomorrow. You understand that you have to count every penny to make every penny count. When you do these things, you can begin to create money—more and more money.

Respect for your money and respect for yourself are linked. Building one builds the other. With the next step, you will learn how much you already know about this process. We all have the wisdom within us that will tell us, if we listen, how to act—with our money and in every aspect of our lives. Getting in touch with that voice from the core of our being is not only a step toward Financial Freedom. It's also a step toward spiritual serenity. That they go hand in hand is not as odd as it may seem at first glance. When you can create money, you are suddenly free to live a life rich in all kinds of ways.

Please make a commitment to yourself to look over your investments this week and make sure they are invested as respectfully as possible.

I promise to look over my investments this week and make sure they are invested as respectfully as possible.

_____	_____	_____
Date you will take action this week	Signature	Today's date

STEP 6

Trusting Yourself
More Than You Trust Others

When I was a stockbroker it never ceased to amaze me that I could buy the exact same stocks for my clients and some clients would always make money and others would never make money.

When brokers find stocks they like, they try to do what is called building a position in the stock—buying lots of it for their clients. For instance, if I liked Widget stock, I'd call every single client I had to tell him or her about Widget.

Then I'd say: "How many shares would you like, five hundred or one thousand?" I was taught in stockbroker training school never to ask a yes-or-no question when trying to make a sale. By asking in a pointed way whether clients want five hundred or one thousand shares, you leave them with only a choice of how many shares they want, not whether they want any at all.

I was a good salesperson, so most of my clients would buy Widget at, let's say, $85 a share. Now let's suppose all of a sudden Widget cut its dividend, and before you knew it, the stock was down to $40 a share. My phone would begin ringing off the hook. Some people would invariably say, "Sell! Sell! I don't want to lose more than half my money!" In those cases I had no choice but to sell the stock. Some of my other clients, in for a longer haul, might not have been happy that the stock was down to $40 but still knew that this was a good company and that in time it could come back. Often they would buy more shares at the lower price. Before you knew it, Widget was at $120 a share. All of my clients had bought the same stock. Some had made money, and some had lost it. By the way, if you think I'm exaggerating the way stocks move, I'm not. Something very much like this happened with IBM stock in the late 1980s.

It also worked the other way around. Let's say this time I was building a position in Lobster Pots. All my clients bought the stock at $6 a share, and before long it went up to $12 a share. Big increase. I'd call my clients and some would say, "Okay, sell it." Others would say, "Let me think about it," then call back to say, "No, let's see if it will go a little higher." All of a sudden something happened and the stock fell, to $4 a share. All the people who didn't want to sell it at $12 now got frightened and sold at a loss.

Over the years I started to notice that the people who lost money in both of these cases were always the same people. They'd sell too soon or too late, but they'd always lose money. In the business, we called them clients with "the kiss of death" when it came to their investments.

It bothered me when my clients lost money, and I began to think about it. Finally I realized that it wasn't a matter of luck, but a matter of, well, spirit, for lack of a better word. It was the attitude, the instinct, with which the client went into an investment that helped to determine whether he or she would make money or lose money. Of course there are good investments and bad investments. But however solid the investment, the investor has to be solidly behind his or her investment to make money.

I began to see, too, that the questions I had been taught to ask as a broker worked very well for me—I was rich in commissions—but often worked less well for my clients. I changed my approach. I began really talking to my clients about how they felt about investing in the stock market in the first place. The ones who invariably lost money said that it made them nervous, that they didn't like it. I asked them why, then, they invested in stocks, when there were so many other excellent places to put their money, and their answer changed my life: "Because you told me to, Suze." They were trusting me more than they trusted themselves.

From then on, my heart just wasn't in selling stocks the way it had been. I can date the beginning of my financial advisory practice to the moment I asked my first client, and then my second and third, how they felt about buying a stock, rather than asking whether they wanted five hundred or one thousand shares. If there was any hesitation whatsoever, I began to suggest that clients pass. I suggested that they pay attention to that little voice inside them, because what it was telling them was what was right for them to do. In 1987 I left the corporate brokerage world to start my own firm, where I could really give advice that was good for my clients, not just good for me. Now I give advice in my books that is good for anyone with financial concerns.

> **THE FIFTH LAW OF FINANCIAL FREEDOM:**
> You and Your Money Must Keep
> Good Company

There are many ways the universe offers us guidance to protect ourselves, but we usually just turn our backs on this guidance because we don't recognize it as such. The little voice inside you is actually a powerful signal. I believe it's the voice of God, and if you listen to it, and take action based on what it tells you to do, it will keep you safe and sound. This sixth step to Financial Freedom is about finding that voice inside you and learning to listen to what it has to say when it comes to your money.

> **THE SIXTH LAW OF FINANCIAL FREEDOM:**
> Inner Trust First,
> Then Outward Action

LISTENING TO YOUR VOICE

Never forget this: You will never be powerful in life until you are powerful over your own money.

I am not telling you not to seek out a financial advisor. All I am saying is that if you decide to go that route, you need to know without a shadow of a doubt whose best interest your financial advisor has at heart. It really is that simple.

DO YOU HAVE A FINANCIAL ADVISOR OR A SALESPERSON?

If you are using a financial advisor, please answer yes or no to the following questions:

	YES	NO
Do you pay commissions to buy your mutual funds?	_____	_____
Do you own a variable annuity within your retirement account?	_____	_____
Has your financial advisor ever sold a mutual fund you owned within the first year of your owning it and bought another one?	_____	_____
Has your advisor ever made a transaction in your account without your permission?	_____	_____
Has your advisor ever asked you to write a check to him or her personally when you were buying a stock, bond, or mutual fund?	_____	_____
Did your advisor leave you completely alone during the market decline of 2000 and 2001?	_____	_____

Look at your answers. If you answered yes to the majority of the questions, there is a good chance you have a financial advisor who is nothing more than a salesperson.

✓

I hope you are seeing that there is an inherent danger when financial advisors' paychecks are dependent on whether you buy what they tell you is good for you. How many commission-oriented advisors would encourage you to invest money in a way that avoided a commission? Not many, in my opinion. And you will see there are many ways to do just that—invest wisely without paying unnecessary commission fees.

On the following page there is a chart with a brief overview of the different ways financial advisors make money.

QUICK REFERENCE GUIDE:
HOW DOES YOUR FINANCIAL ADVISOR MAKE HIS OR HER MONEY?

Fee Only	Commission/Fee	Commission Only	As a Money Manager
You pay the advisor an hourly fee or a set fee to tell you what to do with your money. The advisor simply advises you, and you are responsible for managing your money and funding your accounts.	You pay the advisor a fee to tell you what to do, to create a plan for your money. If you decide you'd like the advisor to implement the plan for you, he or she will get a commission over and above the fee.	The advisor gives you advice for free in the hope you will follow that advice by buying the recommended investments through him or her. If you do make a purchase, the advisor makes money on commissions. If you do not make a purchase, the advisor makes no money at all.	The advisor manages your money on an ongoing basis for a fee that is usually a percentage of the money you've given him or her to manage ($50,000 and up, with the average being around $200,000). This percentage can range from 0.25% to 3% a year, but you should not pay more than 1.5%, including all commissions.

Buyer Beware: The Basics of Choosing a Financial Advisor

Below is a list of what to look for and what to avoid in a financial advisor.

1. Any financial advisor who calls you cold—whom you don't know and have never heard of—should be sent packing. Hang up. A successful advisor doesn't have to look for clients. Clients seek him or her out.

2. If an advisor has time to come to your home, something is probably wrong. When I was seeing clients—long before I wrote my first book—I didn't have time to breathe, let alone get in a car and drive across town to a client's home and then drive back again.

3. You should make it a point to visit a potential advisor's office, in any case. You'll want to pay careful attention to how the advisor keeps his or her professional space. Is it busy? Is it neat? Do the files seem to be in order?

4. If you are married or have a life partner, a potential advisor should have found this fact out by asking and should see you only if you agree to bring your partner along.

5. A good financial advisor will ask you all—not some, but all—of the following questions: How is your health? (This is number one, since if you're not healthy you'll need first and

foremost to plan for your medical care and possibly your income if and when you cannot work.) Are you in debt? (This is number two.) Are you responsible for aging parents? Are you saving for your children's education? Do you have a will or trust? Will you inherit money someday? Do you need to make a major purchase like a new car, or a new roof for your home? Do you have a retirement plan? Are you funding the plan to the maximum allowed by law? Do you have adequate insurance? Only after an advisor fully understands your financial situation should he or she ask you how much money you have to invest.

6. An advisor should be a Certified Financial Planner®, or CFP® professional. That means that he or she cares enough about his or her clients to have gone through a two-year certification process, with continuing education requirements mandating that he or she stay up to date on the kinds of information that you need.

7. You should be told up front how, and how much, a potential advisor will be paid. You shouldn't have to ask. *The correct method of payment is by fee only.* Any advisor who wants to be paid through commissions charged on the investments he or she makes for you has an incentive to move you in and out of stocks and other investments, perhaps in direct opposition to what's best for you.

8. An advisor should never ask you to write a check to him or her. You should write checks only to a brokerage firm, an insurance company, or another financial services firm.

If You Aready Have a Financial Advisor

If you currently have a financial advisor, you should make sure that he or she is fulfilling each and every one of the following expectations. If the advisor you are using falls short, do yourself a favor and get yourself a new advisor, or better yet, try managing and investing your money on your own.

1. She will call you every time she makes a change in your account.

2. He will explain in detail why he wants you to agree to each and every new transaction.

3. She will explain every commission.

4. He will never pressure you into doing anything that does not feel right to you.

5. She will send you a transaction slip from the brokerage firm that holds your money, telling you what has been bought or sold. This slip must always match transactions for which you gave permission.

6. He will never ask you to make out a check to him personally. All the money that is handed over should be made out to an institution.

7. She will return your calls in a timely manner.

8. He will prepare both quarterly reports and annual reports that will tell you the exact return he is getting on your money AFTER all fees and commissions have been taken out. This is in addition to the monthly statements that the brokerage firm should be sending you.

9. She will keep you informed about your money, not just call you when she wants you to buy or sell something.

10. If you already have an advisor, that advisor should be calling you in down markets as well as in up markets. Has your advisor called you within the past twelve months?

11. She will direct all information to both you and your life partner and take into consideration how you both feel about your jointly held money.

THE BEST FINANCIAL ADVISOR IS YOU

Nobody is going to care about your money more than you do. And what happens to your money is only going to affect the quality of your life—not my life, not your broker's life, but your life. So you have to educate yourself. Once you've been educated, if you feel you need an advisor go find one. You should make sure the financial advisor has experienced a bear market, as in 2000–2001, along with a bull market, that he or she really has your best interests at heart, and that he or she asks questions that make sense—not just about how much money you have, but other ones, too: "Do you have credit card debt?" "Do you own your home outright?" "Do you need to make a major purchase?" "Are you going to inherit money?" "Are you going to support your parents?" All these questions should be asked, and it should feel right for you. If it doesn't, he or she is not a good financial advisor. Advisors you interview must spend a lot of time, at least a couple of hours, getting to know you and your money. They can't simply take your answers from a questionnaire, plug them into a computer, and give you a plan. What needs to be built is a responsible, respectful, and trusting relationship, and you must not settle for less.

On the next page is a questionnaire I used to review with my clients. It outlines the concerns any prospective advisor you interview must address. If you are your own financial advisor, it is essential that you also fill out this worksheet for yourself. If you decide to work with a financial advisor, please fill out this worksheet prior to meeting with the advisor so you have a checklist of what should be asked, along with the information to provide your advisor.

WHAT THE ADVISOR MUST ASK YOU OR YOU MUST ASK IF THE ADVISOR IS YOU

Name: _____ Partner's name: _____

Address: _____

Phone number: _____

Occupation: _____ Occupation: _____

Retirement date: _____ Retirement date: _____

Will you get a pension? _____ Will you get a pension? _____

Retirement plan: _____ Retirement plan: _____

Any loans against a
   retirement plan? _____

Any loans against a
   retirement plan? _____

Will you get Social Security? _____ Will you get Social Security? _____

Is this your first marriage? _____ Is this your first marriage? _____

If not, what number is it? _____ If not, what number is it? _____

Is your ex still alive? _____ Is your ex still alive? _____

If you are receiving income from him/her at all, If you are receiving income from him/her at all,
   does it stop on his/her death? _____   does it stop on his/her death? _____

If you want to invest some money, for how long are you certain, without a shadow of a doubt, that
   you can let it stand without touching it? _____

Age: _____ Age: _____

Health status:* _____ Health status:* _____

*The financial advisor needs to know about your health. Will your health prevent you from working? Do you need to plan for large medical expenses? Will you qualify for LTC insurance or health insurance? This is a key question. If your financial advisor has never asked you about your health or the health of your loved ones, you should think twice about using him or her.

Are parents alive? _____ Are parents alive? _____

If not, cause and age of death: _____ If not, cause and age of death: _____

Are they divorced/separated? _____ Are they divorced/separated? _____

Mother's age/health:* _____ Mother's age/health:* _____

Father's age/health:* _____ Father's age/health:* _____

*A good financial advisor should ask about the health of your parents and your life partner's parents to determine whether you are going to have to take care of them emotionally and financially.

Goals

By the time you leave the office today, what is it that you want to have learned? (Couples, please list your goals separately.)

Partner A: _____

_____

_____

Partner B: _____

_____

_____

Dreams

Do you have any dreams that you would love to see come true (to be answered by both partners, if in a couple)?

Partner A: _____

_____

_____

Partner B: _____

_____

_____

Do you think they will come true?

Partner A: _____

Partner B: _____

Emotional Quotient*

* A financial advisor needs to know what makes you feel powerful or not—if, for example, you are afraid you will buy and sell at the wrong time. Investing is about making you comfortable, not just about making more money for you.

Do you get nervous when you think about investing in stocks? _____

If you were to buy a stock at $15 a share and it went down to $10, how would you react, as rated on the scale below?

I'd lose sleep and be sick to my stomach	I'd check the papers daily when investing in stocks	I'd think, "That's what happens"

10   9   8   7   6   5   4   3   2   1

Cash Flow

List all sources of income that you have now and that you expect to have when you retire.

_____

_____

Write down two years' expenses so we can see what you really spend, compared to what you think you spend. _____

_____

_____

Security

Do you/your partner have disability insurance? _____

Do you/your partner have errors-and-omissions or malpractice insurance (if applicable)?

_____

What are the deductible and coverage on your car insurance, house insurance, and health insurance? _____

_____

_____

_____

How long have you/your partner worked at your current occupation/s?_____

_____

Do you/your partner like your current occupation/s?_____

Do you/your partner plan a career change in the foreseeable future? _____

At what ages do you/your partner want to retire? _____

Has your company downsized in the past ten years? _____

Family

Parents

All of the questions apply to both sets of parents.

Do you have open communication with your parents about their money?_____

Will you be inheriting any money from your parents? _____

If your parents need physical or financial help, will you be the one responsible for them?

_____

Are you or any family member willing to move them into your home if they need help?

_____

Do your parents have an LTC insurance policy? _____

Do your parents have a will or trust and a durable power of attorney for health care?

_____

Are both of your parents citizens of the United States? _____

If not, why not?_____

_____

Children

Names:_____

Ages:_____

Are your children dependent upon you financially?_____

How long do you anticipate that they will be financially dependent?_____

Do you have any children currently on Supplemental Security Income?_____

Do you have any children on Social Security Disability?_____

Do any of your children have (or have a history of) a substance abuse problem?_____

Will you be paying for their college education?_____

Have you started to save for their college education?_____

Do they think you will be paying for their college education?_____

Are you willing to sacrifice your retirement security in order to pay for your children's education? _____

Are you opposed to your child having to pay for his or her own education?_____

Have you paid for any of the other children's education at this point in time?_____

Do you talk freely with your children about money?_____

Do you feel that if you were to die today, they would be capable of handling the money you are going to leave them?_____

If not, at what age do you feel you would let them get control of this money, if ever? _____

Do you feel that you want someone else to watch over the money for your children, and, if so, until they are how old? _____

Real Estate

Home

Do you own a home? _____

What is the fair market value (FMV) of that home today? _____

What was the purchase price of the home? _____

Before this home, did you own a home or homes that you sold? _____

Did you roll your taxable gains (from the sale of your home or homes) into your current home? _____

If so, what was the purchase price of the first house that you started with? _____

Have you kept records of all the home improvements that you have made to this home or any prior homes? _____

If no records were kept, can you estimate the cost of improvements on all homes to date? _____

What is the balance that you owe on the mortgage? _____

What is the interest rate? _____

Is it a fixed or a variable loan? _____

How many years do you have left until it is paid off? _____

Do you have a home equity loan or second mortgage on this home? _____

What is the balance remaining on that loan? _____

What is the interest rate of that loan? _____

Do you plan on keeping your current house?_____

If not, how long before you sell it? _____

If you sell it, will you be buying another one? _____

How much will you want to spend? _____

Other Real Estate

Do you own any other real estate? If yes, please answer the following questions for each piece of property owned:

What kind of property is it (apartment building, commercial property, rental unit, second home, vacation home, etc.)? _____

What is the FMV of that piece of real estate? _____

What was the purchase price? _____

Did you own other similar real estate that you sold to buy this property? _____

Did you roll your taxable gains into this property? _____

What was the purchase price of the first property that you started with? _____

What is the balance that you owe on the mortgage? _____

What is the interest rate?_____

Is it a fixed or a variable loan? _____

How many years do you have left until it is paid off? _____

Do you have an equity loan or second mortgage on this property?_____

What is the balance remaining on that loan? _____

What is the interest rate of that loan?_____

Do you plan to keep this property? _____

If not, how long before you sell it? _____

If you sell it, will you be buying another one? _____

How much will you want to spend? _____

TOTAL EQUITY IN ALL REAL ESTATE OWNED (FMV minus all mortgages and all equity loans): _____

Debts*

A financial advisor should ask about debt because he or she needs to know if you would be better off paying your debt than investing in the stock market.

Car

Do you owe any money on a car or have a car loan? _____

	Car A:	**Car B:**	**Car C:**
Balance of loan	_____	_____	_____
Interest rate	_____	_____	_____
Years remaining on loan	_____	_____	_____
Do you plan on selling any of these cars?	_____	_____	_____
If so, when?	_____	_____	_____

Credit Cards

(begin with the one charging the highest interest rate)

	Amount Owing	**Interest Rate**	**Yearly Fee**
Card #1 _____	_____	_____	_____
Card #2 _____	_____	_____	_____
Card #3 _____	_____	_____	_____
Card #4 _____	_____	_____	_____

School Loans

_____	_____	_____	_____
_____	_____	_____	_____

Personal Loans

_____	_____	_____	_____
_____	_____	_____	_____

Credit Union Loans

_____	_____	_____	_____
_____	_____	_____	_____

TOTAL CURRENT DEBT:

_____

Anticipated Debt*

Will you be making any large purchases in the next two years (buying a new car, a new roof, or a computer; taking a vacation; etc.)? Please list the item and the amount you expect to spend.

Item	Amount
_____	_____
_____	_____
_____	_____
_____	_____

*It is critical that your financial advisor know about your anticipated debt. If you'll need money in the near future, you should not be investing that money.

TOTAL ANTICIPATED DEBT: _____

Add up your current debt and anticipated debt.

Cash on Hand (available at any time with or without penalty)

	Current Balance	Interest Rate	Monthly Income
Savings account	_____	_____	_____
Checking account	_____	_____	_____
Money market funds	_____	_____	_____
Credit union	_____	_____	_____
Other	_____	_____	_____

TOTAL CASH ON HAND: _____

Cash-type Investments

	Current Value	Interest Rate	Maturity Date	Monthly Income
Certificates of deposit	_____	_____	_____	_____
Treasury bills	_____	_____	_____	_____
Other	_____	_____	_____	_____

TOTAL CASH-TYPE INVESTMENTS: _____

Other Investments

	Current Value	Interest Rate	Maturity Date	Monthly Income
Mutual funds	_____	_____	_____	_____
Stocks	_____	_____	_____	_____
Bonds	_____	_____	_____	_____
Annuities	_____	_____	_____	_____
Stock options	_____	_____	_____	_____

TOTAL OTHER INVESTMENTS:

Money in Retirement Accounts

	Current Value	Return	Company Match	Monthly Income
Traditional IRA	_____	_____	_____	_____
Roth IRA	_____	_____	_____	_____
SEP	_____	_____	_____	_____
Keogh	_____	_____	_____	_____
403(b)	_____	_____	_____	_____
401(k)	_____	_____	_____	_____
Tax Sheltered Annuity	_____	_____	_____	_____
Other	_____	_____	_____	_____

TOTAL RETIREMENT ACCOUNTS:

Life Insurance Policies

Company	Owner of Policy	Cash Value	Current Interest Rate	Death Benefit
_____	_____	_____	_____	_____
_____	_____	_____	_____	_____
_____	_____	_____	_____	_____
_____	_____	_____	_____	_____

TOTAL LIFE INSURANCE CASH VALUE:

TOTAL LIFE INSURANCE DEATH BENEFIT:

Now add all the following:

TOTAL EQUITY IN ALL REAL ESTATE OWNED (page 133): _____

TOTAL CASH ON HAND (page 135): _____

TOTAL CASH-TYPE INVESTMENTS (page 135): _____

TOTAL OTHER INVESTMENTS (page 136): _____

TOTAL RETIREMENT ACCOUNTS (page 136): _____

TOTAL LIFE INSURANCE CASH VALUE (page 136): _____

EQUALS TOTAL ASSETS: _____

Subtract from that:

TOTAL CURRENT DEBT (page 134): _____

EQUALS NET WORTH: _____

✓

MAKING YOUR MONEY WORK FOR YOU

Now that you know that the key element in making sure that you have Financial Freedom is *you,* I want you to try to start investing on your own. Even if you use a financial advisor, why not take just a small amount of money and invest it by yourself? You just might be shocked to find that you made more money on your own than by relying on your advisor. The best and easiest way to start is by utilizing mutual funds. To begin, this is what you need to know.

What Is a Mutual Fund?

A mutual fund starts out as a pool of money into which many investors just like you have put their money. The manager or managers of the fund take all this money and put it into different investments. The manager or team of managers decides what to buy and sell, based on personal judgment and research by many others.

Each mutual fund invests in a unique selection of stocks, bonds, and other investments, and the goal of each fund is different. Some invest for long-term growth, some for income, some for a combination of the two. Some invest here in the United States and some invest only overseas. The variations go on and on, but if you have a specific interest, I guarantee that you can find a mutual fund that addresses it.

Basically, when you invest in a mutual fund you own a tiny fraction of each share of stock or whatever the fund manager has purchased. So even if you own just one mutual fund, your money is still quite diversified, because you own a little of everything the fund has invested in.

If you had a financial advisor at a full-service brokerage firm, he or she would have to consult you before making any transactions, and you would have to pay a commission almost every time you bought or sold anything. That's not the case with a mutual fund, where the manager has free rein over the money in the fund and you're not charged a commission when transactions are made. You will receive a prospectus and information with a breakdown of what the mutual fund has been up to, but you're not notified day to day. By buying shares in the fund, you have made the decision to trust the fund manager based on his or her track record.

A good mutual fund is a great way to invest money, particularly small sums of money. You achieve diversification, commission-free trading within the account, and a professional manager or team of managers who are buying and selling and doing what they think best.

With Thousands of Mutual Funds Available, How Do I Choose?

You can buy mutual funds that invest in almost anything you want. Once you decide on your goals, you now have three choices: Do you buy a managed mutual fund, an index fund, or an exchange-traded fund? On the following page you will find a quick reference guide to the different types of mutual funds.

QUICK REFERENCE GUIDE:
DIFFERENT TYPES OF MUTUAL FUNDS

	Managed Funds	**Index Funds**	**Exchange-Traded Funds**
What is the difference?	A managed fund is run by a manager or team of managers who decide what to buy and sell with all the money investors have deposited in the fund. In a sense, you're investing in the manager who's in charge of the fund.	An index fund is simply a mutual fund that buys the entire index (or group of stocks and bonds) that it is tracking. Indexes include, for example, the Standard & Poor's 500 index, Nasdaq, the Wilshire 5000 equity index, and the Russell 2000 index.	An exchange-traded fund combines the features of an index fund with those of a stock. When you buy an ETF you are buying units in a trust that holds stocks in proportion to their weightings in the index the fund is duplicating. Like managed funds, ETFs offer a level of diversification that would be difficult for you to achieve on your own or through outright ownership of stocks.
Do I need to research the man-ager of the mutual fund?	Yes. If you know what kinds of things you'd like to invest in, you should find a like-minded manager and choose that fund, if its track record stands up to scrutiny. Look to see how long the manager has been in charge. Is the current manager the one responsible for a fund's terrific track record, or has that person moved on, leaving someone new in charge?	No. Index funds have a portfolio man-ager, but the manager simply buys the entire index that the fund is duplicating, such as the S & P 500 index.	No. Like an index fund, the ETF trust portfolio is passively managed, moving up and down as the stocks on the index move; the manager has little discre-tion. To find out more about ETFs, go to the American Stock Exchange Web site, www.amex.com.
Which type is best?	Very few managed funds have out-performed the S&P 500 index. In addition, they have management fees and end-of-the-year capital gains tax distribution.	Index funds do not have management fees or end-of-the-year capital gains tax distribution. Many of the good index funds require a high initial deposit ($3,000) to open an account. Two of my favorite index funds at this writing are. Vanguard 500 Index Fund Symbol: VFNIX (800) 662-7447 Vanguard Total Stock Market Index Fund Symbol: VTSMX (800) 662-7447	ETFs have very low management fees and no end-of-year capital gains dis-tribution. Unlike most index funds, they do not require a high initial deposit to open an account. If you want, you can buy one share, which could cost you as little as $100.

Load Fund, No-Load Fund, or 12(b)1 Fund: What's the Difference?

When mutual funds first came on the scene, you could buy one only through a broker, so they were all "load" funds. Over the years, though, many mutual fund companies came out with "no-load" funds, which do not charge a commission to purchase them. Slowly but surely investors began to see the value of no-load funds. The difference between a load fund with a commission and a no-load fund without a commission is about 4.5 percent, give or take, out of your pocket. 12(b)1 funds are sometimes presented as though they are no-load funds, but they have a hidden load. Please see below.

QUICK REFERENCE GUIDE:
NO-LOAD FUNDS, LOAD FUNDS, AND 12(B)1 FUNDS

No-Load Funds	Load Funds or A Shares	Load Funds, 12(b)1, or B Shares
A no-load mutual fund is a mutual fund you buy without an advisor's or salesperson's aid, and therefore there's no commission attached to it. You know you have a true no-load fund when you see in the newspaper that the sell price and the buy price of the fund are identical. No-load mutual funds are the only way to go.	A load fund is a mutual fund an agent sells you for a fee. This "load" is usually around 5%. Load funds are also known as A share funds. They can usually be detected because they have an A after the name of the fund, and there is a difference between the buy price and the sell price of the fund.	This is my least favorite kind of fund, in that they are usually sold to you by a financial advisor under the pretense that you are not going to have to pay a load as long as you stay in the fund for five to seven years. If you cash out before that time you incur a "surrender charge" starting at around 7% and going down by 1% each year until it reaches 0%. In addition, you will be paying an extra 0.75% to 1% a year in 12(b)1 expenses. This charge, in essence, is what covers the commission the agent was paid by his or her brokerage house to sell this fund to you. 12(b)1 funds usually have a B after their name. Be careful, because they appear to have the same buy price and sell price when you look them up in the papers, but this does not mean that they are true no-load funds. These are the worst types of funds you can buy.

Where Do You Stand with Your Mutual Fund?

To find out where you stand with your mutual fund, please answer yes or no to the following questions:

	YES	NO
Do you know how your current mutual fund compares to its index?	_____	_____
Do you know if it's a load or a no-load mutual fund?	_____	_____
Do you know the expense ratio of your mutual fund?	_____	_____
Do you know the tenure of the fund manager?	_____	_____
Do you know the yearly turnover ratio of your mutual fund?	_____	_____

✓

If you answered yes to all of the questions above, congratulations. Please fill in the chart on the next page to determine how your mutual funds compare to their indexes.

If you answered no, don't get intimidated or frustrated. Knowing how your investments compare to their index is easier than you think. Let's fill in the worksheet on the next page together.

Instructions

To help you evaluate how well your mutual funds are performing, you need to gather some basic information, such as load or no load, expense ratio, turnover ratio, tenure of fund manager, and mutual fund performance compared to the index fund it most resembles. All of this information can be found on Smart Money's Web site. Go to www.smartmoney.com. Click on the blue "funds" box. Enter the fund name or symbol in the box titled "enter name or symbol." Then click on the red arrow. Your fund's "snapshot" screen will appear. It lists the fund's symbol and other pertinent information.

1. List all of the funds that you have in your portfolio on the worksheet on the next page.

2. List each fund's symbol.

3. Now list load/no-load information in the appropriate column on the worksheet. You will find this information on the "snapshot" screen in a section called "Funds Stats."

4. List the expense ratio in the next column. Click on the gray "expense" tab on the tool bar; the expense ratio is listed under the "key numbers" information.

5. Now list the turnover ratio in the appropriate column. Click on the gray "portfolio" tab on the tool bar; the turnover ratio is listed under the "key numbers" information.

6. In the next column, list the tenure of your fund's manager. Click on the gray "snapshot" tab on the tool bar. In the lower part of the screen, you will find the "Funds Stats," including his or her start date.

7. List if your mutual fund has outperformed its index fund over the past year. Click the gray "return" tab on the tool bar; this will take you to a screen that compares your mutual fund to its index fund. In the time period box on the "return" screen, click on one year.

MUTUAL FUND WORKSHEET

Fund Name	Fund Symbol	Load or No Load	Expense Ratio	Turnover Ratio	Tenure of Fund Manager	Has Your Mutual Fund Outperformed Its Index Fund?

How did you do? If your mutual fund did not outperform its index, you need to evaluate whether you should make some changes in your portfolio or leave it as it is.

✓

Mutual Fund Information on the Web

Below are some of my favorite sites for information on mutual funds.

www.personalfund.com
This site will help you find the information on fees and the effect they will have on your fund's performance.

www.smartmoney.com
This site has daily mutual fund recommendations and personal finance research tools.

www.quicken.com
Quicken has basic information and research tools to help you find and evaluate mutual funds.

www.fundmaster.com
You can request a free annual report and prospectus of any mutual fund you are interested in from this site.

www.indexfundsonline.com
This site presents all the options available in index funds.

www.fundalarm.com
Fundalarm keeps track of what is going on in your mutual fund and sends you an alarm to bring important fund news to your attention.

www.ici.org
ICI Mutual Fund Connection is a good place to continue your education on how mutual funds work.

www.vanguard.com
This is a great educational site on the subject of mutual funds.

www.morningstar.com
The site contains state-of-the-art information, ratings, and research tools on mutual funds.

GETTING READY TO INVEST

It doesn't matter whether you have a lump sum you want to invest or are starting from scratch and want to put in a little here, a little there. Rule number one is that to invest in the stock market (this includes mutual funds, index funds, and individual stocks), you must invest only money that you will not need to touch for ten years or longer. Why? Because, there has never been in the history of the stock market a ten-year period in which stocks have not outperformed every single other investment you could have made.

Not that history always repeats itself, but this is a spectacular indicator—investing in the stock market is a really great bet. However, if you do not give your money ten years, you will be taking a significant risk. That's because, in shorter periods of time, stock prices and fund values go up and down.

If you don't have ten years to leave your money in the market, it is possible that when you do need to take it out, the need will arise at the worst possible time. Let's say you invested in 1999 and were planning to withdraw the money to buy a house within the next four years. You decided, "OK, I'll just invest in the market, make all I can, and then have money when the time comes to make the down payment." One year later you find the house you want and make the offer, which is accepted. That day the market goes down considerably. You would most likely take out far less than you put in. You wouldn't be able to wait for the market to go up again because you needed the money to buy your house. As you see, timing is everything.

INVESTMENT QUIZ

You have $10,000 to invest. Which guaranteed return would you want? Please pick one.

_____ A. A guaranteed return of 80 percent increase on the first year but a 50 percent loss on the second.

_____ B. A guaranteed return of a 5 percent increase on the first year and a 5 percent increase on the second.

Most of you would reason that if you got 80 percent the first year and lost 50 percent the second year, you would still be up 30 percent. So most likely you would choose A, because 30 percent is still better than 5 percent one year and 5 percent the second. Yet if you answered A you would be wrong.

In order to be a successful investor you have got to understand how numbers work. If you start with $10,000 and you make 80 percent in year one, you have made $8,000 and have $18,000 total. If you lose 50 percent of the $18,000 in year two, or $9,000, then the total you have left would be only $9,000. You now have $1,000 less than when you started two years ago, or 10 percent less.

In the second scenario, if you started with $10,000 and made 5 percent you would have made $500 and would have $10,500 total at the end of year one. In year two, you would have made another 5 percent, or $525, for a total of $11,025. Thus scenario B would give you $2,000 more than scenario A.

DOLLAR COST AVERAGING—THE KEY TO SMART INVESTING

When you're ready to invest your money you will want to use a technique called dollar cost averaging. With dollar cost averaging, you are investing a portion of your money every month and in that way averaging the price of whatever shares you're buying over time. It puts time, your money, and the market on your side. Since you are investing every month, you hope to buy into your funds when the market is going down, so you don't have to pay so much for your shares. When this happens, you will be paying less per share and so will be able to buy more shares. Then, when the market goes up again, you will own more shares to profit from. When you begin paying yourself every month in this way—just as you do with a retirement plan—not only do you get more long-term bang for your buck, you also take some of the risk out of investing this money.

By using the dollar cost averaging technique, even if you are investing for the long run (ten years or more), in the end you will end up a winner.

EXAMPLE OF HOW DOLLAR COST AVERAGING WORKS

Afraid of a falling market? With dollar cost averaging, you benefit.

	Monthly Dollar Contribution	Price per Share	Number of Shares Bought
January	$750	$15	50.00
February	750	15	50.00
March	750	12	62.50
April	750	14	53.57
May	750	12	62.50
June	750	13	57.69
July	750	12	62.50
August	750	11	68.18
September	750	10	75.00
October	750	10	75.00
November	750	9	83.33
December	750	10	75.00

Total invested: $9,000
Shares bought: 775.27

Look at what happened to the shares: In twelve months they dropped 33 percent in value, from 15 down to 10. By dollar cost averaging, you bought 775.27 shares, for which you paid $9,000. At the current price of $10 a share, your investment is worth a total of $7,752.70, for a paper loss of $1,247.

Now, if you had taken that same $9,000 and invested it at the January rate of $15, you would have had only 600 shares and they would now be worth only $6,000, for a loss of $3,000 rather than $1,247. Then, as the share price started to increase again, you would own 175.27 fewer shares to reap the profits from.

When Do I Buy?

To dollar cost average, take your monthly investment sum and, on the same day each month, put it into a good no-load mutual fund. You are going to contribute the same amount month in and month out for the first year, using the dollar cost averaging technique. Please fill in your monthly amount on the worksheet on page 147 and compute your dollar cost average every month for the next twelve months.

You have a choice when it comes to buying mutual funds or index funds. You can buy them directly through the fund company itself, or you can open an account at Charles Schwab, Fidelity, Muriel Siebert, or any of the other major companies and buy the same no-load funds through the discount broker. (Make sure there is no transaction fee involved; there shouldn't be.) Schwab and Fidelity, among others, have pamphlets and computer programs to help you select the best mutual funds for you. There is more good help for you out there than you can imagine.

Some of the great families of funds:

Fidelity	(800) 544-9797	www.fidelity.com
PIMCO	(949) 720-6000	www.pimco.com
Janus	(800) 525-3713	www.janus.com
T. Rowe Price	(800) 638-5660	www.troweprice.com
TIAA-CREF	(800) 842-2252	www.tiaa-cref.org
Vanguard	(800) 662-7447	www.vanguard.com

DOLLAR COST AVERAGE WORKSHEET

Month	Monthly Dollar Contribution	Price per Share	Number of Shares Bought
January			
February			
March			
April			
May			
June			
July			
August			
September			
October			
November			
December			

✓

What Do I Buy?

What you buy will depend in part on how much you have to invest, because some funds have a very low minimum initial deposit requirement, while with others you need to invest more up front. The minimum will also vary depending on whether you're investing in a retirement account or on your own in a regular account. The Vanguard Group, for instance, which is one of the great mutual fund companies, has a minimum of $3,000 if you open just a regular account. If you open an IRA at Vanguard, the minimum drops to $500. Most mutual funds work more or less the same way, although a few good no-load funds will let you invest with minimums as low as $50 to $100, if you allow the fund to deduct a similar amount from your bank account each month. They're smart; they just want you to start, and then continue to save. These include:

Fremont Funds	(800) 548-4539	www.fremontfunds.com
Invesco	(800) 525-8085	www.invesco.com
Neuberger & Berman	(800) 877-9700	www.nbfunds.com
Strong Funds	(800) 368-1030	www.strongfunds.com
T. Rowe Price	(800) 638-5660	www.troweprice.com
TIAA-CREF	(800) 842-2252	www.tiaa-cref.org

Plunging in Deeper?

If you are serious about testing the investment waters, you may want to join a fabulous organization called the American Association of Individual Investors (www.aaii.org). This entity has been around since 1978, now has about 175,000 members—independent investors like you—and costs $49 for paper membership or $39 for electronic membership. It will send you information that, believe it or not, you will enjoy reading; its information is always thorough and good.

Once you have invested for a year, you may decide, as thousands of other people have, that yes, you're perfectly safe on your own. If you find it heady and exhilarating, if it makes you feel both safe and powerful, then by all means plunge in deeper. Watch carefully over what you are creating, keep in mind your time frame, and always listen to your inner voice.

If, instead, after this first year of investing you find you're not comfortable with it and your inner voice says that you would rather have professional help before you plunge in deeper, then you must listen to that voice. And you must find the very best help you possibly can.

TEACH YOUR CHILDREN WELL

Remember how, in the beginning of this guidebook, you went back to your own childhood and began to reconstruct your money memories in order to understand how they led to your fears about money today? So, too, are your children becoming imprinted with money memories right now. It is your responsibility as a parent—or aunt, godparent, or friend of a child—to give careful thought to how you transmit messages about money to the children in your life.

Over the past few years a small industry has arisen to produce books, games, and computer programs to teach children about money. If you have a child, buy as many of these as you can and pull the best ideas and information from them. The advice won't be the same—that's OK. Again, follow your inner voice about what and how you want your kids to learn. The best things about these books and products is that they open up a dialogue about money, a subject that has been treated as a secret for too long. But they can go only so far, because money messages are transmitted as much through the heart as through words in a book or images on a screen. If your kids hear you swear at your stack of bills, they sense fear; if they're constantly told what you can't afford, that's what they'll learn. We relay messages of fear many times over to our children, especially when it comes to college funding. In order to send our kids to school, the bank truly has to be broken wide open.

Saving for Children's Education

The cost of a four-year college tends to rise at about 5 percent a year, while inflation currently seems to be holding steady at about 2 percent.

Child's Age in September 2002	Projected Cost of In-State Public University or College (5% inflation)		Projected Cost of Private University or College (5% inflation)	
18 (Sept. 2002 enrollment)	$54,789/4 years	or $13,697/year	$118,050/4 years	or $29,513/year
13 (Sept. 2007 enrollment)	$69,927/4 years	or $17,482/year	$150,665/4 years	or $37,666/year
8 (Sept. 2012 enrollment)	$89,246/4 years	or $22,312/year	$192,291/4 years	or $48,073/year
1 (Sept. 2019 enrollment)	$125,578/4 years	or $31,395/year	$270,573/4 years	or $67,643/year

Financial Freedom means more than just having a lot of money; it also means being proud of what you have, being realistic about what you don't have, and instilling that pride and sense of realism in your children. To go into debt forever to pay for an education is not being respectful of yourself or your money. Greatness will come into a child's life regardless of where he or she gets an education, because true greatness starts from within, not from without. True greatness and true education start with the messages that are passed down, the conscious messages and the unconscious ones.

How Will I Afford College?

If the numbers in the chart above seem staggering, don't let them stagger you. Try to make decisions today about education tomorrow that will be respectful of you and your children. The sooner you start saving the better. The chart below shows the big difference a few years can make.

AMOUNT NEEDED TO SAVE TO HAVE $200,000 FOR COLLEGE

Age Investing Begins	Monthly Amount (at 9% annual return)
Start investing when born	$366
Start investing when eight years old	$633

I believe buying stocks, especially growth mutual funds, is the best way to invest for long-term growth. However, anytime you're considering an investment, how soon you will actually need that money is critical to choosing the right investment vehicles.

Years Before College	Risk Level	Portfolio
10 +	Aggressive	Aggressive mutual funds
6–10	Moderate	Conservative mutual funds
4–5	Conservative	High-yield money market funds Treasury notes CDs EE bonds

Education Provisions of the Tax Relief Act of 2001

The Economic Growth and Tax Relief Reconciliation Act of 2001 created approximately $29 billion in direct tax and savings incentives for education expenses. Let's review some of the options that are now open to you.

Education IRA

The Education IRA was something I was never excited about because the previous annual contribution limit was only $500. As of 2002, the annual limit has been raised to $2,000, transforming this IRA into an effective savings vehicle. And the new law has created other benefits as well:

- Starting in 2002, for the first time ever, your contributions to an Education IRA and the earnings the account generates can be used to pay for qualified educational expenses for grades K–12 as well as for college. Moreover, qualified expenses now include tuition, academic tutoring, special-needs services, books, supplies, room and board, uniforms, transportation, supplementary items or services (such as extended-day programs), and the purchase of computer technology, equipment, and Internet access. (Computer software primarily involving sports, games, or hobbies is not considered a qualified school expense unless it is educational in nature.)
- Although the money you contribute is still not tax-deductible, as of 2002 the earnings will be tax-free if spent on qualified educational expenses.
- As of 2002, using money from an Education IRA will no longer disqualify you from taking a Hope Scholarship or a Lifetime Learning credit in the same year, as long as the Education IRA money and the tax credits are not used for the same expenses.
- Starting in 2002, the income cap to qualify for an Education IRA will go up to $110,000 for single filers and $220,000 for married joint filers (from $95,000 and $150,000, respectively, in 2001). Contributions can now be made until April 15 of the year *following* the year for which the contribution is designated (instead of December 31 of the designated tax year, as under the old law).

- For special-needs beneficiaries, contributions can be made to accounts after the beneficiary reaches age eighteen. The new law also makes it clear that corporations and other entities (including tax-exempt organizations) are permitted to make contributions to Education IRAs, regardless of the income of the corporation or entity during the year of the contribution.
- You can now make a contribution to an Education IRA in the same year that you or a friend or relative makes a contribution for the same beneficiary to a qualified state tuition program. Please keep in mind that *distributions* from an Education IRA and a qualified tuition program cannot exceed the beneficiary's qualified higher-education expenses for any year. Any *distribution* in excess of qualified expenses must be returned to the contributor by May 31 of the following tax year or taxes will be imposed.

For these reasons, I have now switched from not liking the Education IRA as an education savings program to liking it very much.

Section 529 Plans

Section 529 plans have always been excellent tools to use to save for college, but the Tax Relief Act of 2001 has made them even better. One of the best provisions is that, starting in 2002, any earnings that accumulate in a Section 529 college-savings plan will be income-tax-free when used to pay qualified expenses for a child's higher education. Qualified expenses include tuition, fees, room and board, and books. But please be aware that if the current tax law stays as written, in the year 2011 a sunset provision will kick in. This means that if you withdraw funds from a 529 plan in 2011 or later, the money will be taxed at the tax rate of the person using it, just as it was in 2001.

In the meantime, there are many, many additional benefits:

- You can participate in a Section 529 plan no matter what your household income, and caps on annual and total contributions are comparatively high. Depending on the state and the program you choose, 529 plans allow contributions ranging from $15 per month to a total of $250,000, over time or at once. As to federal limits, people who file their taxes singly may contribute up to $50,000 and married couples filing jointly may contribute up to $100,000 all at once, without incurring a gift tax (assuming there haven't been or won't be other gifts to the same beneficiary within five years).
- Contributions can be used at any college or graduate school you choose—private or public; in state or out of state.
- Unlike Uniform Gifts to Minors Act (UGMA) or Uniform Transfers to Minors Act (UTMA) accounts, 529-plan accounts are controlled by the individuals (typically parents or grandparents) who set them up and not by the beneficiaries. But they are gen-

erally not included in the owners' estates for estate-tax purposes. In addition, distributions are excluded from gross income if used to pay for qualified higher-education expenses—meaning that you pay no taxes on earnings in the account if you use them for qualified expenses.

• Some states allow residents to deduct their contributions on their state tax returns.

• The new law allows you greater flexibility. You have the ability to spread your investment over several state plans, if you choose. And with the new tax law, you can roll money from one state-sponsored plan to another, as often as once a year, if you feel that your money might grow faster in another plan; the new law eliminated the rule that required plans to impose a penalty on any withdrawals and replaced it with one that imposes a 10 percent tax penalty on withdrawals not used for qualified educational expenses. And if your child changes his mind about going to college or gets a scholarship, the new law even allows you to now transfer the money in a plan to another beneficiary who is a first cousin, say, rather than to immediate family members, as the old law did.

• Finally, as with Education IRAs, taxpayers who receive distributions from a qualified tuition plan beginning in 2002 will also be eligible to claim either the HOPE or the Lifetime Learning credit in the same year, as long as the plan distributions are not used for the same expenses for which a credit is claimed.

Right now, plans are primarily available through state institutions. But the law has been modified to include what are called "prepaid tuition programs" established and maintained by private institutions—although tax-free withdrawals from private prepaid plans won't begin until 2004. Please keep in mind that private educational institutions must first receive a favorable IRS ruling, and program assets must be held in a trust. Still, bottom line: You *can* now purchase tuition credits or certificates for beneficiaries from private institutions.

There are two general types of Section 529 plans—prepaid tuition plans and college savings plans. With either one, you are no longer limited to using the money for just state schools or schools in the state plan. The states that offer prepaid tuition contracts covering in-state tuition will allow you to transfer the value of your contract to private and out-of-state schools (although you may not get the full value; that depends on the state). If you decide to use a college savings plan, the full value of your account can be used at any accredited college or university in the country, or even at some foreign institutions.

In other words, 529 plans are excellent saving programs. For more information on Section 529 plans and the new tax bill's effect on them, you can visit Joseph Hurley's Web site, www.savingforcollege.com.

By the way, given the new tax advantage for Section 529 plans, there is now no reason whatsoever to save for college via a UGMA or a UTMA account. In my opinion, these accounts are now obsolete.

The Higher Education Deduction

The Tax Relief Act of 2001 created another wonderful benefit: a tax deduction for higher-education expenses. Please note that you cannot take this deduction and the HOPE or Lifetime Learning credit in the same year.

Adjusted Gross Income Not Greater Than $65,000 ($130,000 for Joint Filers)		Adjusted Gross Income Over $65,000 But Not Greater Than $80,000 ($160,000 for Joint Filers)	
Year	Maximum Annual Deduction	Year	Maximum Annual Deduction
2002–2003	$3,000	2002–2003	n/a
2004–2005	$4,000	2004–2005	$2,000

To determine if you should take the higher-education deduction or the HOPE Scholarship or the Lifetime Learning credit, you need to evaluate which benefit gives you the greater tax relief.

Employer-Provided Educational Assistance

The Tax Relief Act of 2001 also extends what's called the employee exclusion from income of employer-provided educational assistance, meaning that you won't pay income tax on education benefits your employer provides. The educational assistance amount is up to $5,250 and can cover tuition, fees, books, and supplies, but not room and board. Education does not have to be work related, but the employer must maintain the program. This provision was scheduled to expire but is now permanent and includes graduate school expenses, which have not qualified for the exclusion since 1996.

Student Loan Interest Deductions

Another benefit of the new law: Student loan interest on qualified educational or refinanced educational loans can be deducted from your taxable income—though you cannot claim this deduction if you are claimed as a dependent on another person's tax return for that year. The maximum annual deduction is $2,500. Where the old law allowed just the first sixty months of interest payments to be deducted, in the new law there is no time limit. And there are no restrictions concerning voluntary interest payments while the loan is deferred or in forbearance. Married, joint filers whose adjusted gross income is not above $100,000 and single filers whose adjusted gross income is not above $50,000 can deduct the full amount of interest paid each year (not to exceed $2,500). Married, joint filers with adjusted gross incomes between $100,000 and $130,000 and single filers with adjusted gross income between $50,000 and $65,000 can deduct a portion of the interest paid. These income levels are to be adjusted annually for inflation.

The HOPE Scholarship Credit and Lifetime Learning Credit

The HOPE Scholarship was created to help with the cost of education for students in the first two years of college (or other eligible post-secondary training). With the HOPE, if you qualify you can deduct $1,500 a year directly from your income-tax bill for every college freshman and sophomore in the family. (A credit is not deducted from your income; it is deducted *directly from the amount of tax you owe,* and therefore is far more valuable.) The HOPE Scholarship credit is divided into two parts: you can deduct 100 percent of the first $1,000 of tuition and fees and 50 percent of the second $1,000 (the amounts are indexed for inflation after 2002). The credit is available on a per-student basis for net tuition and fees (less grant aid) paid for college enrollment. It is phased out for joint filers between $80,000 and $100,000 in income, and for single filers with between $40,000 and $50,000. The credit can be claimed in two taxable years (but not beyond the year when the student completes the first two years of college) for any individual enrolled on at least a half-time basis for any portion of the year. The Tax Relief Act of 2001 allows you to take the HOPE Scholarship credit for the same year as you take a withdrawal from an Education IRA or Section 529 savings plan, as long as the withdrawal distribution is not used for the same qualified educational expenses for which the credit is being claimed.

When the HOPE Scholarship runs out, the Lifetime Learning credit kicks in. Designed for those beyond the first two years of college, or those taking classes part-time to improve or upgrade their job skills, it lets the family claim a tax credit equal to 20 percent of the first $5,000 in qualified educational expenses, for a total maximum credit of $1,000 (20 percent of $5,000). Starting in 2003, the maximum gets better: The credit will increase to 20 percent of the first $10,000 in qualified expenses, for a total of $2,000. (These expense limits will not be indexed for inflation.) The credit is per family, not per student. It applies to all the children for whom you're paying out-of-pocket educational expenses. It is available for net tuition and fees (less grant aid) for undergraduate and graduate school and has no limit on the number of years it can be taken. The Tax Relief Act of 2001 allows the Lifetime Learning credit to be claimed in the same year that a withdrawal from an Education IRA or Section 529 plan is taken, as long as the withdrawal distribution is not used for the same qualified educational expenses for which the credit is being claimed. Like the HOPE Scholarship, the Lifetime Learning credit is phased out for joint filers with between $80,000 and $100,000 in income and for single filers with between $40,000 and $50,000. Unfortunately, married taxpayers filing separately are not eligible.

EDUCATIONAL SAVINGS OPTIONS

	Section 529 Plan	Unified Gift to Minors Act Account	Education IRA	Roth IRA
What is the difference?	A Section 529 plan is a state-run, tax-deferred savings plan, sponsored by a state and managed by a reputable bank, mutual fund company, or investment management company, specifically designed for saving for college. The account is owned by the adult who set up the plan and not by the future student. For more information, visit: www.savingforcollege.com.	Under UGMA, money is held in trust for your child. The money does not have to be used for educational purposes and it belongs to the child once he or she turns either 18 or 21, depending upon the state.	An Education IRA is designated for saving for college; contributions are not tax-deductible, though as of 2002, earnings are tax-free if used for qualified expenses. Education IRA savings do not impact on the maximum contributions allowed for other IRAs.	Although contributions to a Roth IRA are not tax-deductible, a Roth allows you to take your original contributions out at any time without taxes or penalties. Roth IRA funds do not need to be designated for college expenses. For more information, go to www.rothira.com.
How much can you contribute?	With most state plans, you can contribute up to about $100,000 to $150,000 per student per year. Programs allow funding ranging from $15 per month to a total of $250,000, over time or at once.	Not limited.	You can contribute up to $2,000 a year in your child's name.	Year / Under Age 50 / Over Age 50: 2002–04 $3,000 $3,500; 2005 4,000 4,500; 2006 4,000 5,000; 2007 4,000 5,000; 2008 5,000 6,000. After 2008, increases will be indexed in $500 increments based upon inflation.
How is it taxed?	As long as withdrawals are used for qualified educational expenses before 2011, earnings in the account are never subject to federal income tax and are mostly exempt from state income tax as well. Non-qualified withdrawals are subject to a 10% penalty tax on the amount of the distribution that is includable in the recipient's gross income.	The first $750 of earned income is taxed in the child's zero tax bracket (if not over 14 and with no other income); the next $750 of unearned income is taxed at 10%, and the rest is taxed at the parents' tax rate if the child is under 14.	Earnings are tax-free when used for college expenses.	Contributions are taxed but earnings grow tax-free. Original contributions can be withdrawn penalty-free at any time. You can also withdraw your earnings penalty-free for educational purposes, but you will have to pay ordinary income taxes on the earnings withdrawn if you are not at least 59½ at the time of the withdrawal.
Are there any income restrictions?	There is no income restriction. Up to $50,000 by singles or $100,000 by married, joint filers may be contributed at once without incurring a gift tax (assuming no other gifts to the same beneficiary within five years).	There are no income restrictions.	Yes. Starting in 2002, the income cap to qualify for an Education IRA will go up to $110,000 for single filers and $220,000 for married, joint filers.	Yes. If your adjusted gross income is $95,000 or less for single filers or $150,000 or less for married, joint filers, you can contribute the full amount per year. Lesser amounts can be contributed for AGI under $110,000 for singles and $160,000 for married, joint filers.

How Prepared Are You to Help Fund Your Child's College Education?

Please answer yes or no to the following questions:

	YES	NO
Do you want to help contribute toward the cost of your child's college?	_____	_____
Are you able to contribute monthly to a college-savings plan?	_____	_____
Will there still be enough money to go on contributing to your retirement plan?	_____	_____

If you answered yes to the questions above, you need to begin actively saving for your child's college. In order to do this, you need to be realistic about the costs and how much you can contribute. Please ask yourself the following questions:

How many years until my child goes to college?

What have I saved to date to contribute toward my child's college education?

Is there a monthly amount that I can contribute starting today?

With this basic information in mind, you must begin contributing this month. To determine how much you will need to contribute, please input your numbers into the various college financial calculators available on the Internet. At one of my favorite Web sites, www.finaid.org, you will find various financial calculators as well as college-cost projections. Be realistic about what you can contribute while still saving for your retirement. If you want to contribute to your child's college education, the earlier you begin saving the better.

If you want to contribute but do not know where you are going to come up with the extra money, the first thing you need to do is review the worksheet "Deciding How I Choose to Spend My Money" on page 35. You will need to decide which categories you are willing to trim.

✓

Additional Financial Aid Resources

www.finaid.org
Here you will find just about everything you will need, including calculators to help you do math on loan payments, college-cost projections, financial aid estimation forms, reference book resources, videotape resources, and information on free booklets by mail, periodicals, and lobbying and advocacy groups and discussion groups.

www.collegesavings.org
Another useful site on saving for college.

Federal Student Aid
(800) 4-FED-AID
www.fafsa.ed.gov

The free application form can be used to apply for most state loan, grant, and scholarship programs, in addition to the federal loans and grants. When you submit the FAFSA to the U.S. Department of Education, the department forwards the information on the form to the state student assistance agency. You must submit the FAFSA every year that you want to receive federal aid. The FAFSA is available in paper and electronic formats. You can get the paper version from your high school, the financial aid office at any college or university, the public library, or by calling the toll-free number listed above. Or fill out an online version of the FAFSA at the Web site listed above (step-by-step instructions are provided at this site).

YOUR CHILDREN'S REAL EDUCATION

College notwithstanding, your children's real education about money will take place all through their childhood; it will occur in the way you talk about money, in the way you present what working is all about, in the way they learn what they have a right to hope for in this world.

Children can absorb a lot, if you will just trust yourself and open up to them. Play money games with them, using mail-order catalogs and price tags in stores to teach them value. When they're old enough, tell them about your 401(k), your strategies for investing, and what this all means in the context of their young lives. Rather than a traditional passbook savings account, give your children a little money in a mutual fund and let them keep careful watch over it. Talk to your children about how the world presented in advertisements, with a stunning array of things to consume, is different from the real world. Turn the dinner table conversation to the subject of money, and talk to your children about what it means to save for college, for example. Explain what credit cards are, and what you're doing when you go to the bank, and what the cash machine is all about. Talk about what it means to be poor. Talk about what it means to be rich. Talk about charity, and let your children see your charitable efforts in action often. Talk about prices, and values, at the supermarket. Talk about mortgages, and debt, and insurance, and how you make choices about money. By talking to your children about money, you will be talking to them about the way the world really works, and teaching them valuable lessons.

ON TRUSTING YOURSELF

With this sixth step toward Financial Freedom, you have learned to trust yourself more than you trust others. Now you must watch over all that you have begun to create.

Whether you are managing your money yourself, have handed its management over to an advisor, or have chosen a combination, you must know exactly how your money is doing at all times. Remember, not only must you trust yourself, you must also be respectful of yourself and your money.

You can keep track of your financial life any way you want, but you must do it, studying all statements carefully and keeping watch in between. The easiest way to do this is by signing up for an online service like America Online, which, if you choose to have it do so, will automatically value your portfolio and tell you exactly how much you are up or down every time you connect into it. Make checking your mutual funds and any other investments you own a part of reading the paper every day. It can be a pleasurable part of your day: you are creating wealth. Your wealth.

With these last three steps we have covered the vital forces that will help you open the door to Financial Freedom.

- You must be responsible to those you love.
- You must be respectful of yourself and your money.
- You must trust yourself more than you trust others.

Once you have taken these steps in their entirety, you have blown the door to Financial Freedom off its hinges. You will then be in a position to walk through that door. The next step, the seventh step to Financial Freedom, guarantees that you will not unintentionally limit what is to be found on the other side.

STEP 7

Being Open to Receive All That You Are Meant to Have

By now you've completed all the hard work, the Must-Dos of Money. You've learned how to become a money magnet. You've learned about trusts and wills, the insurance you should and should not have, credit card debt, saving for retirement, choosing a financial advisor, mutual funds. While those steps are more demanding on a practical level, the final three steps to Financial Freedom are lighter, shorter, and yet profoundly potent. So after spending the last six steps hiking uphill, now it's time for you to coast a little. Enjoy where these last three steps take you.

Congratulations for staying committed to your goal of attaining Financial Freedom. I promise you, you will reap the rewards of completing these steps. I've seen it many times before. People's lives have literally been transformed after they've completed all these steps. The fact that you're here with me on Step 7 tells me that you are well on your way to great fortune of all kinds. For those of you who are on Step 7 but did not do all the exercises prior to this step, you'll get something out of Step 7 but chances are you will not attain true Financial Freedom. I urge you to go back and do all the exercises. Don't take a shortcut. Don't rip yourself off.

In this step we're going to explore what it means to be open to receive all that you are meant to have. I want you to think about those words. Is it just possible that you're doing something in your life that is blocking all the money that's meant to come your way? I'm going to tell you, it's not just possible, it's probable.

Suze's Story

When I was starting out as a commissioned broker, I never knew for sure if I would make money the next month or not. I'd freeze in a panic. The more I froze, the more depressed I felt, and sure enough, suddenly there was nothing I felt enthusiastic about buying or selling for my clients.

I remember being in a terrible funk once. I decided to stay home from work for a day and escape by watching TV. I happened to catch one of those PBS fund-raising drives. As I continued to watch, I became really moved by the participants' passion, and I pledged $300. Three hundred dollars seemed like a hefty amount to me at the time, but somehow I felt that it was the right figure.

I can't tell you how good I felt when I hung up the phone. I got up and called a few friends, and I went back to work the next day. Later that week I was in my office, smiling, when Cliff, one of the brokers down the hall, came in and said, "Looks like you're in better spirits. What happened?" This made me stop and think for a moment. I didn't know at first, but then I realized that my mood had switched right after I gave money to PBS.

So every time poverty consciousness hits me and I sink into another money funk, I promptly take out my checkbook and send a check to one or more charities. It is the strangest thing but I feel much better right away. Even stranger: As soon as I feel spunky again, good things begin to happen to me. In every instance, the amount I give is showered back on me tenfold in no time.

After my own experience with PBS and then with other charities, I came up with the theory that to be open to receive you must give to others. Then I started to test my theory with my clients. I went back through my files and divided my clients into two groups, those who gave money on a regular monthly basis and those who did not. What I found was that those who donated regularly had an abundance of money, more than they really needed. Most of the others didn't.

To make sure my theory was correct, I did a little experiment with new clients who weren't doing so well with their money. I asked those I thought would be open to the idea to start donating money each month to a place they felt good about giving to. To new clients that in my opinion wouldn't be open to giving to charity, I said nothing and just did their financial plans as normal. I couldn't believe the results. The better people felt about themselves from giving, and the more they kept their hands open to receive by relinquishing money, the more their financial situation improved. The key was to start respectfully to give money away by making an offering on a regular basis. They had moved to Financial Freedom by giving their money to others.

DO YOU REPEL MONEY?

	YES	NO

Have you ever felt depressed or worried about something important in your life, your work, or your relationships?

If yes, what was the circumstance?

_____

_____

_____

	YES	NO

Did you feel as if you didn't have enough energy to get through the day, even to carry out your ordinary routines, much less to do challenging tasks in your life or your job?

If yes, why do you think you lacked energy?

_____

_____

_____

	YES	NO

When you feel this way, isn't it true that the phone does not ring, the check you've been waiting for doesn't come, even your closest friends seem to vanish for the time being?

If yes, why do you think this happens?

_____

_____

_____

Can you see how, when you are feeling powerless, your whole world kind of crumbles with you? Your money responds to you in the exact same way people do.

When you are feeling powerful in your life, money is attracted to you. It comes to you. Have you ever noticed your mood when you feel powerful? You wake up feeling better and stronger. Once your mood turns around in this direction, everything else does, too. The phone starts to ring. The check arrives. A friend telephones to invite you somewhere nice. When you are feeling powerful in your life, people are attracted to you. It works the same way with you and your money. ✓

MONEY FLOWS THROUGH PEOPLE

As we've seen, money is a living entity and it responds to energy, including yours, and how you feel about yourself.

When you are worrying about money, feeling powerless over your finances, and sorry for yourself, money won't want to hang around you either. On the other hand, when you feel you are in control of your money and have enough to be generous with, money will naturally flow your way. Strange, perhaps, but true. You will become the money magnet that you want to be.

We all spend a lot of energy fussing over our money, wishing for more income, balancing our checkbooks, wondering whether we'll have enough to pay our bills. But there's a question even more important to ask than "Do I have enough?" Is it possible that you are doing something to prevent more money from coming in? Might you be not only the prisoner but also the warden in your financial prison?

What I Learned from the Parrot Seller

I was in Mexico once, and there was a merchant at a market who had many parrots for sale. They were just sitting on perches, none of them in cages, none flying away. I was fascinated by the fact that not one of them was even trying to escape. I asked the merchant, "Do these birds just love you so much they have no desire to fly away?"

He laughed. "No," he said. "I have trained them to think their perches mean safety and security. When they come to think this, they naturally wrap their claws tightly around the perch and don't want to release it. They keep themselves confined, as if they've forgotten they know how to fly."

Suddenly a lightbulb went on. We are, I thought, just like those poor parrots. We have all been taught to clutch our money as tightly as we can, as if our money were the perch of our safety and security. Just like those parrots, we have all forgotten how free we really are—with or without the perch. The more afraid we are, the tighter we hold on, the more we have trapped ourselves.

When I realized this I asked the merchant how he would go about "unteaching" this behavior. "Easy," he said. "You just show them how to release their grip, and they can fly as freely as they want."

Easy for the parrots, maybe. But how, I wondered, do we go about releasing our grip on money?

RECEIVING EXERCISE

Please imagine that you've gone into your kitchen and turned on the faucet. In your imagination, close both your hands in tight fists and try to get a sustaining drink of water from the faucet using just your fists. Obviously you'll have no success quenching your thirst.

Now imagine that you have opened up your hands. Put your cupped hands under the faucet and accept the water flowing freely into them. You'll be able to drink to your heart's content. Your thirst will be satisfied and the thought "not enough" won't even enter your mind.

It Works the Same Way with Your Money ✓

If we are grasping what we have so tightly, we are not open to receive or even notice all that may be trying to flow our way. We must learn to release our grip.

Walk up to the first person you see on the street (an ordinary stranger, not a panhandler) and try to hand that person a dollar bill.

How did the person look at you?

_____

_____

Did he or she take it?

_____

_____

Did he or she say anything at all?

_____

_____

How much anticipation (or dread) did you feel before giving the person the dollar?

_____

_____

Were you able to do it at all?

_____

_____

Now take another dollar bill and enter a place of worship. Locate the donation box and place the dollar in it.

How did you feel this time?

_____

_____

Did you say a prayer as you let that dollar drop?

_____

_____

Did you feel better after making your donation?

_____

_____

Compare how differently you felt after giving each "gift." Most of us feel awkward handing money to a person (and most of us feel awkward being the recipient). Remember, the act of giving is meant to open you up, literally to alter how you feel; its power is rooted in your altered state. Most of us, too, feel a serenity when placing the donation in the box, for such a gift to charity is a pure one without the emotional baggage of giving to an individual.

✓

ARE YOU ATTRACTED TO GENEROSITY?

Please answer the following questions:

Who is the most generous person you personally know?

_____

_____

How do you feel toward this person?

_____

_____

Do you think this person can feel your love and appreciation coming back to replenish him or her?

_____

_____

Is there anyone in your life you consider to be cheap?

_____

_____

How do you feel about this person?

_____

_____

Do you think he or she can sense the way you feel?

_____

_____

✓

CHEAPSKATE QUIZ

Are you a cheapstake? To find out, answer yes or no to the following questions.

	YES	NO
Are you constantly worried that people are trying to take advantage of you and your money?	____	____
Are you unwilling to let money go easily because you're frightened of not having enough?	____	____
Do you think another person would describe you as cheap?	____	____

If you answered no to these questions, no doubt you already give freely, of yourself and your money, and already know freedom in your thoughts, your heart, your soul. If you hesitated over any of these questions, or found yourself answering yes, by freeing up your money in this step, you will also free up your heart.

People who are cheap are more trapped than any of those parrots on perches. Being cheap has nothing to do with how much money you have. You can be rich and cheap, or poor and generous. Cheap people guard their water glasses and hoard what they have, to make sure nothing flows out. New water always has to flow in to keep the water in the glass fresh and useful; otherwise it grows stagnant, like standing water in a pond. People who are cheap are letting their money stagnate. What they are missing is the serenity that money handled responsibly and generously can bring to them.

✓

THE RULES OF GIVING

Why do you give?

You give money away as an offering, a true offering to say thank you. Thank you for what you have, and also for what you don't have. You don't ever give money away to get money. You give money away to open up your hands, to release that grip on your money, to feel generous. When you feel generous, you feel powerful, and powerfulness will attract money to you.

How much do you give?

Decide on an amount of money that you feel you can give away freely every month. Let your inner voice determine the amount you should make as an offering. True giving comes as an impulse, so the amount need not be cast in stone, and it may vary from month to month. All that matters is that the amount be meaningful to you and that it be given with thought, humility, and gratitude.

When do you give?

If you are going to write a check to donate your money, write the check at the beginning of the month and keep it in a special place. Why the beginning of the month? So the act of giving is not an afterthought. By starting your giving at the beginning of every month, you are making yourself and your offering a real priority, an act that will stay with you throughout the month.

Whom do you give to?

I want you to give to a nonprofit charity or your house of worship. The purest gift, the one that truly loosens our cramped clutch on money, is a gift to charity. With this kind of gift, no debt is created, no bondage. Maybe you're just slipping cash into a donation box, and no one will ever know that you have given it. I have found that the most liberating offering of all is one you make to a charity you care deeply about. The one exception that I would like you to consider is if your parents or grandparents are in need. If this is the case and you can give to them with deep humility, so as not to create a reverse bondage, you can give them your offering every month.

Whom do you not give to?

We do not have the same duty to give to our friends, brothers, sisters, or other family members as we do to our parents. Even though you may love the others with all your heart, these are different kinds of relationships. There is a real danger of this gift of money tainting the purity of your love—thus tainting the purity of your intention. Most of us can't open our hands gracefully to give or to receive from family members in a pure way, so I do not recommend making your monthly offerings to family members (other than parents or grandparents in need).

GIVING COMMITMENT

Please make a commitment on the way you are going to start giving that is right for you.

Monthly I will give to:

_____

_____

_____

_____

Amount I will give:

_____

_____

_____

_____

_____   _____   _____
Date I will begin giving   Signature   Today's date

✓

THOUGHTS OF POVERTY ARE BONDS OF POVERTY

Regardless of how much money you have, it is the natural tendency of the mind to think: "I can't give money this month, I don't even have enough money to pay bills." Or, "There are so many things that I need, I lack, I want."

This is precisely the moment to give—to give an amount that is meaningful but realistic. You must break these thoughts of poverty because they are chains that keep you bound to poverty. Mental chains may be invisible, but they imprison you nevertheless. You must and you can break through, overcome, move beyond these mental barriers. You must open your hands. Think of how much you do have, think of others with far less, and give thanks with your gift.

True Financial Freedom is a powerful state of mind, a state of being, and it comes from following all nine steps outlined in this guidebook. When you have reached this seventh step, and you feel free to give from what you have and what you are creating, purely and from the heart, you are nearly free. Can you see that? With your offerings you are participating in the flow of wealth, which, I've discovered, is never-ending. It isn't how much you have that creates a sense of freedom. It's how you feel about what you have, or don't have, that either keeps you prisoner or sets you free—which is the eighth step to Financial Freedom.

STEP 8

Understanding the Ebb and Flow of the Money Cycle

The eighth step to Financial Freedom is about understanding and accepting the natural cycles of money as it ebbs and flows through our lives, sometimes in harmony, sometimes in discord, much like the cycles of our bodies, our planet, and the constant up-and-down movement of the economy you read about in the newspapers.

It is very important to learn to accept that your own money will also have its ups and downs. No matter how carefully you plan—even if you do every financial thing right—money, like other living things, isn't always going to behave in ways you can predict. Sometimes you'll have more than you expected, and at other times money will flow out and you'll have less than you thought. There may be a time when you have money in the stock market and the market goes down dramatically. Or maybe you suddenly inherit a valuable piece of property. Perhaps you are downsized from your job without warning, or given a surprise promotion. You think your financial life is rolling along a certain track and boom, a surprise hits and you're going in a different direction.

These transitions can be exciting, and often scary, but they are all part of the natural cycles of life and money. In Step 8, there are two lessons to remember about these natural ups and downs.

First, you must always take the long view of your financial future. If you have taken the steps outlined in this guidebook, the setbacks you may have today or next year will not keep you from Financial Freedom. In order for you to create what is in your power to create, you must believe that you can and you will do it.

Second—and for some people this may be more difficult to do than anything else I have told you so far—you must believe that everything that happens is positive, if you are willing to let it be.

I know some of you are going to say, "Suze, how can it be a positive thing if my husband leaves me and cleans out my bank account?" "How can it be a positive thing if I lose all my savings in a stock market crash?" Please understand, I am not saying such events won't be tragic and painful; I have been through some of them myself, and I know how hard they can be. But I also have learned that if we are open to them, they can teach us lessons and give us gifts that we would never have found at more comfortable times. Things that seem almost unbearable as they're happening to you can, in the long run, lead to riches you never imagined.

This is a very simple truth with tremendous power. If you can believe that somehow everything happens for the best and hold firm to this belief, especially during troubled times or when you undergo what appear to be setbacks in your life, then you will be able to draw the good out of any situation. You will be looking for the benefit, the hidden treasure, and you will be able to profit from even the toughest experience.

I've heard it said that when you first have a dream for yourself, you think it's totally impossible to achieve. As time goes on, you think it's highly improbable. In the end, you know it was inevitable all along. Remember to remember your power—everything you've learned with these steps to Financial Freedom—and put it all into practice every day, because in the grand scheme of life, you'll never really know how things are meant to turn out until they turn out. And when is that? When they turn out as they're meant to turn out, you'll know it.

I learned this from watching the life of my dad.

My Dad's Story

When I was fourteen, my dad had a little shack under the train station in Chicago where he sold fried chicken. One day the chicken shack burned to the ground, and my dad was left penniless. Because he wasn't properly insured, he had absolutely no money to start up another business. His health was suffering, too; he had developed emphysema from all the smoke he'd inhaled in the fire. Everyone was saying how unlucky my dad had been, and this started to bother me, so I went right up to him and asked him if he was unlucky. "Maybe yes," he said, "maybe no."

One day my dad got a call from a salesman who had been one of his suppliers at the chicken shack. The salesman's meatpacking company was going to give my dad the start-up money to open a new place, and they had even found the perfect location for him as well. I said, "See, Dad? You are lucky after all, aren't you?" Again he just looked at me and said, "Maybe yes, maybe no."

A few months later, Morry's Deli (named after my dad) opened up on Chicago Avenue in downtown Chicago; my brothers and I worked there every day after school. There was always a line out the door, and this time I knew my dad was going to make it. Then one day he came home and said that Northwestern University Medical School was expanding and taking over our space, so we would have to find a new location. Just to check, I said, "I guess we're not so lucky after all, Pops," and he said, "Maybe yes, maybe no."

My dad began to look for a new location. A landlord back in Hyde Park, where the original chicken shack had been, contacted him and said that he had the perfect spot. Everyone was happy because Hyde Park was much easier to get to from where we lived. The day he signed the lease, I felt I had to set the luck record straight, so I said, "I guess this means our luck has changed for the better, right, Dad?" And he said, "Maybe yes, maybe no."

The new store was also a success from the day it opened. But only two years after the store opened, we had another fire. This time, I said outright to my dad that I thought he was the unluckiest man in the world, thinking that he would finally agree. "Maybe yes," he said, "maybe no."

It turned out the fire was caused by an electrical short that had started in the apartment next door. The landlord, knowing that my dad had been doing such great business, put him on notice that he was going to triple the rent after he rebuilt the place. There was no way my dad could afford it, so he began looking for another location. When word got out, a representative from the University of Chicago called and offered my dad a spot right on campus. The spot was perfect, right by the bookstore and a hospital where thousands of people worked, and the rent was affordable. My dad called up the landlord in Hyde Park to say he wasn't moving back in. The landlord was in such shock that he offered him back his spot totally rebuilt, and for less rent than he had been paying before. Now my dad was the one in shock. He took both places.

Soon, with my brother Gary's help, both places were up and running—and successful beyond my father's wildest dreams. For the first time ever, there was enough money—more than enough. My dad knew, too, that my mom would be taken care of after he was gone, and he was proud that Gary would carry on the family business. I went up to him one day as all this was happening and I said, "You know what, Pops? You are one lucky duck." This time, to my utter amazement, he said: "Yep, Suze, you got that right." Not long after that, on June 21, 1981, which was Father's Day, my dad died—in his own eyes a lucky man.

My dad's gift was knowing that good luck and bad luck are always in the eyes of the beholder, and always cycling; rarely does either stop for long in any one place. He was able to see past the present situation, whatever it was, to the future. Another thing about my dad's story: Many of the good things would never have happened if the bad events hadn't happened first. If the second fire hadn't happened, and the landlord hadn't tried to raise the rent, Dad would never have found his store at the university nor gotten a better deal at the Hyde Park store.

UPS AND DOWNS OF MONEY EXERCISE

Please think about your entire financial history. Try to remember the worst things that ever happened to you. Here are a few questions to trigger your memories.

Did you ever not get a job you wanted badly?

Did you ever quit a job or get fired without knowing where your next penny was coming from?

Have you ever lost a lot of money on an investment?

Have you ever had a business deal that you worked hard to put together fall to pieces at the last minute?

Have you ever had a relationship break up and, in addition to the grief you suffered, found yourself also very worried about money?

Have you ever had a friendship end over money?

When and why in your life were you most frightened about money?

Think back to how you felt—tense, afraid, paralyzed, angry, determined to prevail, or whatever the emotions were at the time; there may have been several emotions at once. Remember the entire sequence of events.

What was the crisis itself like?

_____

_____

_____

_____

What happened before the crisis to set it off?

_____

_____

_____

_____

How did the crisis resolve itself?

_____

_____

_____

_____

What elements seemed crucial at the time?

_____

_____

_____

_____

Do those elements still seem important now?

_____

_____

_____

_____

How did the crisis change your life?

_____

_____

_____

_____

Have any gains come from the losses you suffered then?

_____

_____

_____

_____

Did any of your misfortunes turn out, over time, to be the best thing that could possibly have happened to you?

_____

_____

_____

_____

Did the gains come in ways you could never have predicted?

_____

_____

_____

_____

✓

TWO LESSONS ON THE UPS AND DOWNS OF THE MONEY CYCLE

Lesson 1: Always take the long view of your financial future.

Lesson 2: You must believe that everything that happens is positive, if you are willing to let it be so.

REMEMBER TO REMEMBER YOUR POWER

If you want money in your life, then you must welcome it, be open to it, and treat it with respect. Your beliefs and your attitude are what will make you feel rich, free to believe in yourself, knowing that you will take the right actions with your money no matter how much money you have or do not have today and knowing that everything really happens for the best.

As we near the close of your Financial Freedom program—we have just one step left to go—I want to make a request of you. Next time you feel that bad luck has struck you again, I hope you'll remember my dad's simple phrase: "Maybe yes, maybe no." If you can face your misfortune and ask yourself how you can find the gift, the lesson, in what is upsetting you now, then you are rich despite the setback. Now you are only one last step away from true Financial Freedom.

STEP 9

Recognizing True Wealth

Well, can you believe it? You're finally here on your final step to Financial Freedom! Now is the time to answer the question "What is true wealth, true Financial Freedom?" This question is the real bottom line of life and each one of us must address it, regardless of the bottom line that shows up each month on our bank statements.

The quality of our lives does not depend only on how we accumulate, save, and spend our money. Financial Freedom lies in defining ourselves by who and what we are, not by what we do or do not have. You are the person you are right now. We cannot measure our self-worth by our net worth.

There is not one of us who, when we leave this earth, is going to be able to take a penny with us. And when you're on your deathbed, your thoughts are going to be about your memories and loved ones. So it's vital that you take inventory right now of what is really important to you.

Suze's Story

I live in Oakland Hills in California, and a few years ago there was a horrendous fire that destroyed three thousand homes. My home was in the path of this fire, so I was told that we needed to evacuate. I had one hour to fill my car with whatever possessions I wanted to take. I filled up my car not with expensive clothes or electronic equipment but with irreplaceable items that money couldn't buy. The pictures of my family. The possessions that were given to me that maybe cost only a few pennies to buy but that were irreplaceable because of the memories that came with them. My car was filled with memories.

WHAT REALLY MATTERS EXERCISE

Imagine the following: You've been told you have only a few minutes to evacuate your house and in that short period of time you may gather the things that hold the most value for you. What would you take with you?

Look around your house quickly and record what you consider your most valuable possessions.

_____

_____

_____

✓

Were you surprised to see what really has value to you and what really doesn't? I bet when you gave some thought to what truly matters to you, what you chose to bring with you were the items that resonate with meaning and memories, the items that tug at your heartstrings. Those tools your dad wanted you to have when he died. The funny lamp you and your first heartthrob bought when you fell in love and thought, in those days, that anything was possible. Your small daughter's stuffed animals, all lined up on a shelf. Your family photos. Items on which you could never place a price tag. I hope this exercise helped you see that what you deeply value are not things with monetary value.

It's always so amazing to me that we spend so much time wanting things that we can't afford to buy, and when it comes down to the bottom line, those aren't even the things that we treasure in our lives. Do you see, when you start to get your life in perspective, what money can and cannot buy of value? Maybe you've had Financial Freedom all along and you just haven't known it.

HOW YOU DECEIVE YOURSELF EXERCISE

Many of us deceive ourselves about a variety of things, and this self-deception must be erased if we want to experience true Financial Freedom. So we need to identify how we are dishonest with ourselves, and then we must end our game of self-deception and clear the way for real riches.

Ask yourself the following questions:

How do I deceive myself?

_____

_____

_____

Do I deceive myself by thinking that I don't deserve all that I have?

_____

_____

_____

Do I deceive myself by thinking that I have less control over my money than I do?

_____

_____

_____

Do I deceive myself by convincing myself that I can afford my lifestyle, when I can't?

_____

_____

_____

✓

How Suze Deceived Herself

Many years ago I was asked a question: "Suze Orman, how do you deceive yourself?" I wrote down every answer I could think of. But the teacher who asked me this question kept saying that my answers were not correct, and finally she gave me the answer to that question—and the answer for me is the same as it is for each and every one of you. The answer is this: You deceive yourself by thinking you are not perfect. You are perfect regardless of the clothes you wear, the cars you drive, the homes you live in, the schools you send your children to, your job title, or how much you have in the bank. There is not one of us that can take a penny with us. We all go out empty-handed. True wealth is that which can never, ever diminish. Your money will go up and down. Don't let your net worth take your self-worth with it. Always recognize the true wealth you have within.

FIVE LAWS TO LIVE BY

I believe that if you live in accordance with these next five laws of life, true riches of all kinds will come your way.

1. May every thought that you think be etched in fire in the sky for the whole world to see, for in fact it is.

2. May every word that you say be said as if everyone in the world could hear it, for in fact they can.

3. May every deed that you do recoil on top of your head, for in fact it will.

4. May every wish that you wish another be a wish that you wish for yourself, because in fact it is.

5. May everything you do be done as if God himself is doing it, for in fact He is.

Rich or poor your life will touch many other lives, and the way in which it touches them is your choice and will determine the legacy you leave to the world. Please make your legacy a rich one.

CONGRATULATIONS

You have just completed the last of the nine steps to Financial Freedom. It is very important that you complete all the exercises in each of the steps. Remember, just reading about these nine steps will not allow you to attain true Financial Freedom. If there are any exercises you haven't done, you need to ask yourself why. What are you afraid of?

I have seen over and over how dramatically fear affects finances. Fear and destructive emotions will separate you from your money for as long as you let them. But if you move beyond your fear, following the nine steps, step by step, you will see that Financial Freedom is possible, regardless of the amount of money you have at this very minute.

Everyone is born with two wings. One wing is the wing of grace, and this wing is flapping at our sides twenty-four hours a day, seven days a week. The other wing is the wing of self-effort. When the wing of self-effort flaps equally as hard as the wing of grace, then you will have flight. Flight into safety. Safety that is Financial Freedom. Where you do not have to worry about being a bag lady on the street. Where anything and everything is possible. But the choice to flap those wings is up to you. You have what it takes and you have the energy inside you—if you simply put into play the thoughts, the words, and the actions to get those little wings of yours going.

May you know that your inner wealth is far beyond anything that you thought possible. That it has the ability to create external wealth to any degree that you want. I hope you take this guidebook into your hands and into your heart and embark on the journey to true wealth and Financial Freedom.

What Is True Wealth?
What Is Financial Freedom?

We have learned how powerful a force money is, how it can create fears that will, if we let them, paralyze us in this life. And we have learned how to silence those fears and put them behind us. We have learned about the essential right actions—how once we take them, we will put our money and ourselves in step with the natural order of things. Most important, we have learned an essential lesson about abundance—that abundance is in crucial ways a state of mind. Our money will see us through this life. It even has the power to live on after we are gone, blessing the people we love through their lives, too, and even on into generations we will never know.

I hope this guidebook will remind you of the richness and worthiness that have been in your life all along. And I hope, too, that this guidebook will help you to create more wealth, to sustain you and those you love. I hope you've written notes to yourself and marked pages that were particularly useful to you. But this guidebook alone will not make you financially free. Money itself cannot make you financially free. Only you can make yourself financially free, and you can do it and so much more. You have that power.

Now is the time for this guidebook to end and for your future to begin. Believe these lessons; live them, for Financial Freedom is within your reach.

I wish you abundance, joy, and true wealth of all kinds.

> " *TRUE FINANCIAL FREEDOM IS ACHIEVED WHEN YOUR PLEASURE IN SAVING MONEY EQUALS OR EXCEEDS YOUR PLEASURE IN SPENDING IT.* "

FOR UPDATES AND REVISIONS, LOG ONTO

SUZEORMAN.COM

THE #1 *NEW YORK TIMES* BESTSELLER AVAILABLE IN PAPERBACK

The 9 Steps to Financial Freedom is the personal finance classic you can't afford to be without. Let this indispensable book be your guide to a prosperous, worry-free financial future.

Available from Three Rivers Press wherever books are sold.

THREE RIVERS PRESS

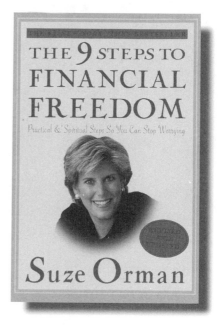

ALSO AVAILABLE FROM SUZE ORMAN